David Hicks
STYLE AND
DESIGN

DAVID HICKS
STYLE AND
DESIGN

VIKING

VIKING

Penguin Books Ltd, Harmondsworth, Middlesex, England
Viking Penguin Inc., 40 West 23rd Street, New York, New York 10010,
U.S.A.
Penguin Books Australia Ltd, Ringwood, Victoria, Australia
Penguin Books Canada Ltd, 2801 John Street, Markham, Ontario,
Canada L3R 1B4
Penguin Books (N.Z.) Ltd, 182–190 Wairau Road, Auckland 10, New
Zealand

First published 1987

Typeset in Linotron 202 Plantin by
Wyvern Typesetting Ltd, Bristol

Printed in Great Britain by
Butler and Tanner Ltd, Frome and London

British Library Cataloguing in Publication Data

Hicks, David, 1929–
Style and Design
1. Interior decoration
I. Title
747   NK2110

ISBN   0–670–80312–X

To Amin and Nahid Ghani, who commissioned the
Vila Verde in the Algarve

ACKNOWLEDGEMENTS

I wish to express my sincere gratitude to:

The Duke and Duchess of Abercorn, Advance Bank Australia Ltd, Lady Cook, Mr and Mrs Amin Ghani, The Lord and Lady Northbourne, Lord and Lady Romsey, The International Wool Secretariat and others, who wish to remain anonymous, who have allowed me to photograph my work for them.

My very real thanks, too, to:

Michael Boys, Norman McGrath, John Miller, Derry Moore, James Mortimer and Fritz von der Schulenburg, who generously gave permission for me to reproduce their splendid photographs.

I would also like to acknowledge the generosity of the editors of Architectural Digest, *American* House and Garden, *British* House and Garden *and* Homes and Gardens, *for allowing me to use material.*

The book would not have been possible without Liz Wilhide's excellent help with the text, Helen Ordish's assistance and the enlightened book design which Nigel Osborne devised.

CONTENTS

INTRODUCTION

This is a textbook about interior design. As the term implies, it will contain much discussion of fundamental principles and a good deal of practical information – from a thorough examination of colour schemes to the best way to disguise a radiator. But the book is also about something much more subjective: taste.

Even in a textbook, it is not possible to lay down rules as to what constitutes good or bad taste. I can give you my views, which are the result of thirty years' experience, and, more importantly, I can suggest a process to help you sharpen your visual sense and come to your own conclusions. For the designer, this process is never-ending. Although I stand by many of the beliefs I formed about design over thirty years ago, there remains much to learn and appreciate. You must always be prepared to welcome and accommodate fresh approaches and new, more skilful solutions.

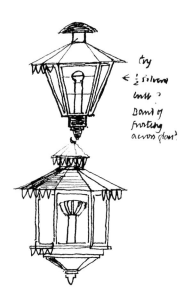

MY DEVELOPMENT AS A DESIGNER

I can vividly recall my first encounter with 'taste'. At the age of twelve I was taken to visit the neighbouring country house of Geoffrey Holme, the editor and proprietor of *The Studio*, an influential magazine that covered all aspects of the fine and applied arts. We went into an enormous library, with a gallery at one end and hundreds of art books lining the walls. There, on a table in the middle of the room, was a model of a cathedral Geoffrey Holme had designed – my eye was just on a level with the floor of the nave. It was magic.

Everything in the house displayed a strong visual sense at work. Objects were massed in collections for maximum effect. Even the garden was exciting and stylish, qualities I had never associated with a garden before. This formative experience taught me how style can be extended to every aspect of life, from the arrangement of a table-top to a flowerbed. The range of interests found in my own career (which has embraced not only the design of interiors but furniture, carpets and textiles, landscape and architecture), can be traced back to the excitement I felt that day.

At the end of the Second World War, when rationing resulted in a period of grim austerity, I had the opportunity to see some rooms that Geoffrey Holme had recently decorated in another house. Despite the shortages, he had created interiors of the utmost luxury. One room had brilliant blue walls, which he had made by adding a blue rinse, which hairdressers use to tint ladies' hair, to ordinary distemper. Against this vivid background he displayed the owners' collection of family portraits and miniatures, their rococo frames painted cream and beige and then rubbed down. With home-made paint and skilful arrangements of existing possessions, he had produced a dazzling effect for next to nothing. It was an important lesson on how little taste has to do with money.

In today's competitive world, most interior designers undertake formal training at art school or technical college. Qualifications are important, but even more vital is any period of relative freedom that can be spent exploring alternatives to the full. For just this reason my time at art school played a crucial part in my development. I studied at the Central School of Art in London, under Keith Vaughan, William Roberts and Jeannetta Cochrane, who was renowned for her theatre and costume designs. I learned to draw, experimenting with the styles of my favourite artists: John Piper, Graham Sutherland and Henry Moore. I read widely about design, visited every exhibition that opened and developed an enthusiasm for the modern architecture of Le Corbusier and Mies van der Rohe.

During this process of exploration, I realized that I would never reach the top in any of the fields I had chosen to study: theatre design, painting, book illustration or typography. What I did discover was a profound and lasting interest in the way people live.

In the early 1950s few 'stately homes' had opened their doors to the public but for five or six years, through the Georgian Group, I was able to visit about fifteen important houses each summer, notably Holkham, Althorp, Chillingham and Mereworth. I steeped myself in the architecture of these historic houses, absorbed the atmosphere of the interiors and gardens and studied every detail. What intrigued me, above all, was the glimpse of other peoples' lives, the way tastes and preferences were expressed in the choice and arrangement of furniture and possessions.

The true beginnings of my career as an interior designer came in 1953 when, after a brief, unhappy stint working in an advertising agency, I set about redecorating the house I had recently bought in London. The whole exercise was one of trial and error. I had no background in the trade and had to start from scratch to find materials and professionals to carry out my ideas. But I knew what I wanted and, although some aspects of the design were imitative, chiefly of John Fowler and the Parisian designer Geffroi, there was enough originality to create an impact.

"Lit an baldaquin"

The most successful room in the house was the dining room, decorated entirely in beige, white and black. The floor was parquet, stained black; the wallpaper, designed by Edward Bawden, had a beige, black and white Gothic design with an octagonal motif. The curtains were white linen with a pennanted pelmet. On the table I put a white linen tablecloth with a bullion fringe; its centrepiece was a white salt-glaze model of a medieval font, octagonal in shape. The only colour in the room came from a basket of green ferns hanging in an alcove in front of the window.

Two other rooms reflected my desire to use colour to 'punch through', a reaction on my part to years of Adam green – which had even percolated through to the barrack rooms of my army days. In the library, I painted the walls matt scarlet and the bookcases black gloss to simulate lacquer. The curtains were cerulean blue felt – at that time furnishing fabrics mainly consisted of insipid chintzes and pale linens, and felt was the only material available in vibrant colours. I also covered a gilt Gothic chair, designed by William Porden for Eaton Hall in the 1820s, with purple felt. Looking back, this was a mistake.

It was also a mistake to put a shocking pink carpet in my bedroom, which already had a collection of Victorian mahogany furniture and an indigo blue on khaki Owen Jones wallpaper that had been specially reprinted. My skill at handling colour has increased over the years, but these first attempts were not only important experiments, they helped to turn me into an interior decorator overnight. When the house was completed, photographs of it appeared in *House and Garden*, and a recommendation by one of its editors led to my first commission, in 1955.

SOURCE MATERIAL

I have described these early influences to highlight some of the sources and inspiration that guided my stylistic development. Whether you intend to embark on a professional career as a decorator or designer, or merely wish to express yourself more creatively in your home, you will need to spend some time developing your own taste.

Today, with new publications on design appearing every week, it is easy to build up a library of source material at home. High-quality reproduction has contributed a great deal to general visual literacy. Start a file of ideas and schemes that interest you, and follow this up by reading widely on the subject.

But however excellent a book or magazine may be there is no substitute for first-hand experience. It is necessary to take the trouble to visit great historic houses and architectural landmarks in order to really appreciate the atmosphere of different periods and the intangible qualities of space, mass and light, none of which reproduce well in two-dimensional form. In the same way, exhibitions of paintings and the decorative arts in general can provide a direct inspiration for colour, shape and pattern. Nature, tamed or wild, is another important source of ideas.

No designer can be effective without a thorough knowledge of what is currently available in terms of professional skills, materials and products. I am fortunate in that my work takes me around the world to every major international centre. Whenever possible I take time to visit design showrooms, investigate manufacturers' ranges and acquaint myself with new trends on the market.

THE QUESTION OF STYLE

There has been something of a boom in the design world over the last decade. In fact, so much has been written about 'style' and so many new ranges have been launched that the whole process of research can become confusing. Many people, faced with such a wealth of choice, take refuge by slavishly copying a 'look', whether contemporary or period. Others assemble a whole host of conflicting ideas, each attractive in themselves, and attempt to put all of them together in one interior. To really emerge with your own consistent approach, your research must be direct and decisive.

The most important lesson I learned during my time at art school was the value of looking 'actively'. Ask yourself what you think about everything you see. Encourage yourself to form opinions – about paintings, the colour of a car, a flower arrangement. Discipline goes hand in hand with good taste.

An early love of modernism, which was my starting point, was a reaction to the Victorian clutter seen everywhere in the over-furnished homes of my parents' generation. My instinct for striking colour combinations arose out of a desire to move away from the restraint of the war years. Today, recoiling from the ugliness and brutality of much of our modern urban environment, I have returned to the past for my inspiration. But this is just a shift in emphasis. Throughout my career I have been interested in reconciling old with new, in combining different strands of interest in a harmonious whole.

Some people remain unaware of what they like, or are unable to come to a decision. I have occasionally had clients who reject all suggestions for a colour scheme but cannot come up with an alternative. In such a situation, I often play a game. I describe the room in question taking the colour scheme from the clothes the client is wearing at the time: for example, grey striped wallpaper, pink curtains, navy carpet. This exercise is not so much a working method as an illustration of the fact that interiors must be an extension of ourselves. A quick glance at your wardrobe will reveal the colours with which you feel most at home; the objects you choose to surround yourself with will give a clue to the textures and patterns you prefer.

Interior design is essentially the process of maximizing the potential of a space and what it contains. The best rooms also have something to say about the people who live in them, telling a story in colour, shape, texture and pattern, that others can appreciate and enjoy.

Below On a tapa cloth from Tonga a nineteenth-century carriage clock sits surprisingly well with a head from Bangkok and three large pieces of Derbyshire spar, the whole arrangement making an interesting composition of textures and surfaces.

CHAPTER ONE

THE WORKING METHOD

This chapter describes in detail the working relationship between client and professional. It examines the progress of a typical job and the type of constraints, financial and otherwise, which may influence the outcome of a scheme. While the information included here is primarily directed at those involved in such a relationship, it applies just as much to anyone who intends to act as their own interior designer.

Even if you decide not to employ a professional designer, the same procedures have to be followed. You have to think about your practical requirements and work out your preferences – in other words, 'brief' yourself. You have to investigate which materials and products are available, and draw up a budget. You have to organize a timetable of work, supervise those you employ and check workmanship.

There is a good deal of satisfaction in designing your own home and, of course, you save the designer's fee. But you also sacrifice one important aspect. In this field, two heads are often better than one and an interplay of ideas can generate more excitement and originality than a single-minded approach. Many people are wary of consulting an interior designer because they do not want a 'look' imposed on their home. This is a misconception: the designer is chiefly a catalyst, who interprets, edits and advises.

It is not easy to play the roles of client and consultant at the same time. Whenever I do a room for myself I realize how difficult this can be – it is another common fallacy that those with a knowledge of decorating do not need the services of a professional themselves. The best way around this problem is to try to work with someone else – a partner, spouse, family member or close friend – who can act as a sounding-board for your ideas and help you define your tastes and needs.

DECORATOR OR DESIGNER?

At the outset an important distinction has to be made between interior decoration and interior design. Interior decoration is, generally speaking, re-covering, re-colouring, re-painting, re-lighting and rearranging an existing room with existing possessions. Interior design is the creation of new interior architecture and form, whether in the conversion of an old building or in a completely new structure. It may involve deciding the position and size of doors, windows and other openings, moving walls and staircases, improving the flow of circulation about the house or changing levels and scale.

In practice, many jobs involve aspects of both decoration and design, but private work for individuals tends more towards decoration, while larger-scale commissions for companies, hotels, offices, restaurants and public buildings offers more scope for design. Very few interior decorators are interior designers, but many designers also decorate. For the sake of simplicity, we will take the broader view here and discuss the subject under the general heading of 'interior design'.

THE DEVELOPMENT OF THE PROFESSION

Interior design is relatively new. In the eighteenth century, architects were responsible not only for the building itself, but were often commissioned to fit out the interior with immovable architectural furniture, or detailing, such as plasterwork and fireplaces. Increasingly, they were also asked to design free-standing furniture as well, formerly the sole province of craftsmen, and also to specify fabrics, floors and wall treatments. A good example is Robert Adam (1728–92), renowned for his architectural achievements, who also designed silverware, carpets, curtains and furniture (some of which was made by Chippendale). Others are Lancelot 'Capability' Brown (1716–83), famous for his landscape designs, who in his later years designed a number of houses, and William Kent (1685–1748), a notable decorator, prolific architect and innovative landscape designer.

Even in the twentieth century, architects have continued to design the interiors of their buildings. Simpson's of Piccadilly, built in 1935–6, contains finishes, rugs, furniture and display stands designed by Joseph Emberton, the architect responsible for the store. The Johnson Wax Company buildings in Racine, Wisconsin (1936–9), designed by Frank Lloyd Wright (1869–1959), feature entire office layouts, including tables, chairs, reception desks and lighting conceived by the architect, and the architect Arne Jacobsen (1902–71), one of the foremost exponents of Danish modern design, was even known to specify the exact positioning of his furniture within the interiors of his buildings. Today, many architects like to retain control over the design of their interiors, but the trend is towards specialization, with qualified interior designers employed on the staff of architectural firms or independent interior designers being retained.

The rise of interior design as a separate profession can be traced to the new prosperity that came with industrialization and with the techniques of mass production that made furniture and furnishings affordable, and so available, to a wider public. A new moneyed class emerged, with spending power but without inherited property or possessions, and a demand grew for advisers who would help create interiors to express this new-found status.

One of the first great interior designers was William Morris (1834–96), a founder of the Arts and Crafts Movement in the late nineteenth century. Many of his wallpaper and fabric designs are still being printed today. During the 1930s, talented amateurs such as Syrie Maugham in England and Elsie de Wolfe in Paris had an enormous impact. Syrie Maugham's passion for all-white rooms was widely imitated; Elsie de Wolfe made many significant contributions that set standards in the new field. It was she, for example, who specified that light switches should be positioned thirty-three inches from the floor. But by far the greatest growth in the profession occurred in the USA; today, Americans are far more likely than the British to use a professional designer when it comes to furnishing and decorating their homes.

The very popularity of interior design and its rapid expansion has led to problems. There have been too many amateurish practitioners who, by foisting unsuitable schemes on their hapless clients, have given the whole business a bad name. The success of major retail outlets in creating 'total looks' that can be assembled by the customer has also contributed to the reluctance of many people to seek professional advice. Yet there are signs that this is changing. With so much choice today, in terms of style, materials and techniques, there is, more than ever, a need for the clear judgement and experience of a professional interior designer, particularly one who works independently of any department store or architectural practice.

TYPES OF CLIENT

There are two spheres of work for the interior designer: the private and the public. Each presents its own challenges and imposes its own conditions.

Private work for individuals normally consists of redecorating, perhaps with an element of redesign, existing rooms using possessions that the client already owns. The approach is necessarily very personal – you are involved in decisions about someone's home, interpreting the way they wish to live and what they would like to say about themselves. At one extreme, I have had private commissions at the beginning of my career that involved no more than recovering two chairs or making a pair of curtains. At the other, I have recently designed a house, designed or advised on its entire contents and landscaped the garden – a breadth of responsibility that is naturally very exciting and fulfilling.

Public commissions are more varied in scope but no less challenging.

Interior designers are often called upon to advise on the fitting out of important common spaces such as foyers, restaurants, showrooms or reception areas, where the commercial client wishes to project a certain image to his customers. But equally often, a designer may just as well be involved behind the scenes, devising offices or boardrooms which will only be seen and used by the firm's staff.

In this field the emphasis is on function. If the purpose of a space is to sell a product or service, the practical requirements of display and presentation come to the fore. If the designer is equipping a reception area, it is important to project the identity of the company as well as create an efficient and welcoming point for visitors. Perhaps one of the most demanding commissions, and one that combines elements of both private and public work, is the design of a restaurant. Here the need for utility and comfort is matched by the need for a certain theatricality. You not only have to consider where to place work-stations and tables, how to regulate the flow of traffic to and from the kitchen, and distinguish the entrance from the main dining area, you must also create a heightened sense that contributes to the experience of dining out. At the same time you must respect the individual needs of customers, treating each table as a relatively 'private' area within a larger arena.

There is another way to categorize clients, and that is in terms of approach. Part of the job of an interior designer is to generate enthusiasm and establish a rapport with the people with whom he or she deals: in other words, to exercise a degree of salesmanship. But the relationship between client and consultant is a two-sided one and it can sometimes go wrong. There may be no common ground at all between what a client wants and what you are prepared to do on his or her behalf; occasionally there may just be a clash of personalities. In such a case, the only solution is to bow out. Happily such circumstances are rare; with the majority, establishing a rapport is a gradual process that begins with the brief.

Far left The Duke and Duchess of Abercorn's rotunda in Northern Ireland is used as a dining room. Lit by a skylight, it has a magnificent coffered ceiling which I painted in three tones of grey. The background of the frieze was painted lettuce green to complement the scagliola columns. The circular carpet, designed to my specifications, was made in the Far East.

This villa in Portugal represents the most comprehensive commission of my career because I was the architect, the interior designer, commissioned the paintings and drawings and designed the furniture for specific positions.

Right The eastern portico, approached by an imposing flight of steps flanked by nineteenth-century gun dogs.

Far right Classical in form, the exterior of the house has roughly rendered walls which·form a pleasing contrast to the plain stone-painted plaster of the columns and window surrounds. The render is composed of orange sand, crushed sea shells, and particles of stone and terracotta.

Right and far right The entrance hall has a geometric floor composed of octagons of bush-hammered stone surrounded by limed teak and punctuated by squares of brown glazed tiles. A pair of magnificent gold and white looking-glasses, c. 1750, from Croome Court, flank the door to the 'big room'. The rest of the wall space is hung with a series of splatterwork silhouettes of ferns dating from about 1860. The two red granite-topped plaster tripod tables can seat twenty people for a large dinner party.

Below right Plan of entrance hall/dining room.

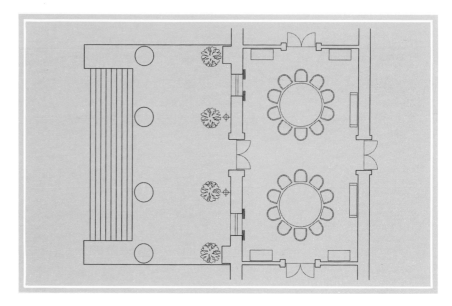

Previous page The loggia, pool and, in the distance, the Atlantic Ocean.

Above right A corner of the big room showing a fine, early-eighteenth-century marble fireplace and one of four magnificent landscapes by Rib Bloomfield, specially commissioned for the room; all are loosely based on the landscape of the Algarve coast.

Below right The design of the sofa fabric was devised from Persian motifs and printed in gold, white and beige pigment on a heavy bronze texture. Behind is a collection of nineteenth-century Algarve aubergine pottery. An antique carved marble horse's head is displayed proudly on a five-foot bronze column.

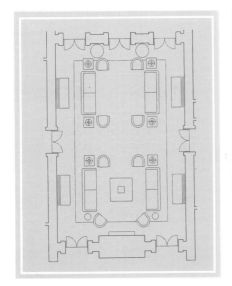

The big room at dusk shows the effect of picture lights, parabolic spotlights and table lamps. The lighting was designed to be dramatic as well as practical. The walls are covered with stretched natural artist's canvas. There are no curtains, as the loggia is always lit at night. The polished-stone floor is covered with a large Brussels-weave carpet of Persian design, which I devised in pale blue, stone, yellow, pink and bronze.

Far left In the dining room a group of Staffordshire pottery figures reflects the figures in the fine Venetian view over the English fireplace, a splendid eighteenth-century example in painted and carved wood. The walls are apple green and the floor is covered in jute matting. Double doors give access to the big room and architectural engravings are hung on the walls. The dining chairs are modern Portuguese reproductions of English-style Portuguese chairs; they are made of local wood with a limed finish.

Above left The pink card-room adjoins the entrance hall. The dark red and white marble fireplace is English Egyptian, from 1825. A large sheet of mirror has been placed above it, and masks from Venice in perspex boxes are displayed on the chimney shelf. In the centre of the room is a circular table with caryatids, under a fine eighteenth-century English crystal chandelier. To the left and right of the fireplace, I devised large Egyptian-style bookcases, which house hi-fi equipment as well as books.

Below left Unlined pure-silk taffeta curtains in tête de negre filter the light. There are four French elbow chairs in the room: two covered in Indian embroidered cloth and two in melon-coloured silk. The carpet has a small geometric pattern of my design in yellow, pink and white. For the walls, a special wallpaper was printed, matching the colour of the lining of an envelope that the client received two years previously. Massed on the walls, like postage stamps in an album, are 200 black and white engravings taken from an illustrated encyclopedia of the early 1800s.

Right Another visitors' room is decorated entirely in different whites. The walls are painted, the floor is covered with cord carpet and inexpensive, local pure cotton is used for the curtains, upholstery and bed treatment. Apart from two coloured prints on either side of the desk, the walls are hung with black and white drawings.

Below and bottom right The main stairway divides and rejoins itself. White plasterwork and white balusters, late-seventeenth-century in design, contrast with the gun-metal stippled wallpaper. A collection of English and Portuguese watering cans is displayed en route to the west garden. Above are various architectural details from the Bahamas and Britain; on the polished local-marble floor are baskets full of kindling and logs.

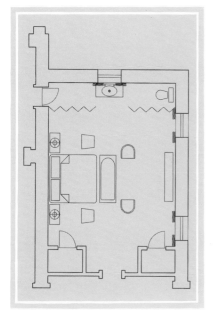

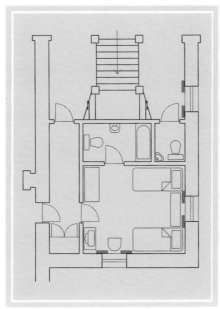

Plans of the visitors' rooms.

Left The ground-floor visitors' room has a polished terrazo floor, laid in a single sheet. The bath, with its red granite surround, stands conveniently at the foot of the bed and in front of the Louis XVI marblized pottery fireplace. The four-poster bed is lined in white and hung with a brown, beige and white floral design of German origin. To the left of the bed is a Persian tablecloth. The cruciform hanging of the engravings of obelisks conceals a jib door. The blinds are left permanently down to protect a fine set of hand-coloured Directoire engravings dating from 1814.

BECOMING ESTABLISHED

There is an element of luck in every successful career and it is most needed at the outset, when one is unknown and untried. Timing is also crucial. I began to work as an interior designer in the aftermath of the Second World War. Since wars inevitably stimulate sweeping changes in society, it was an auspicious time both to launch a career and introduce new ideas.

First clients are very important. After my house appeared in *House and Garden*, I was contacted by Mrs Rex Benson, the American wife of a banker, and formerly the wife of Condé Nast, the founder and proprietor of *House and Garden* as well as *Vogue*. Mrs Benson was direct in her request: 'I'd like to see your house,' she told me. 'I've used Syrie Maugham, Elsie Mendel, John Fowler and Ronald Fleming, and now I want someone new.' As an American, she was accustomed to working

Above The bed in this fabric-lined suite is positioned in the centre of the sleeping area. Light is filtered by day and supplied by two bedside lamps on tables by night.

Left The main suite, comprising bathroom, bedroom and boudoir, runs the entire length of Vila Verde.

Far right The Grange was a Covent Garden restaurant I designed for the film director John Schlesinger; the name suggested an early-eighteenth-century theme for the design. The design of the bar was taken from a seventeenth-century tomb. Portraits framed in stainless steel date from the Biedermeier period in Germany.
Parabolic spotlight downlighters and candles give a dramatic welcoming light.

with decorators and I soon discovered that she had excellent taste. The Bensons owned an attractive collection of period furniture, and good objects and pictures, a palette of possessions that made an interesting beginning. We got on very well together and the job became a joint venture.

In the library, the starting point for the scheme was a Pontremolli needlework carpet, with big roses and leaves on a black background. Taking the colour from one of the roses, I painted the walls red. The bookcases had imposing 'Greek tombstone' style pediments, and the effect was striking.

The drawing room called for a gentler approach. Here I took my cue from the paintings, which were delicate studies by the English couturier and amateur painter, Edward Molyneux. The room was decorated in off-white, with muted touches of colour. Since the room was very high and none of the pictures was large, I introduced a huge screen, ten feet high, with eight panels, each two feet wide, to provide a sense of scale. The screen was covered in white ribbed silk studded with bronze nails and it was positioned where it would also work to reduce the impact of the grand piano – not in front as a disguise, but behind, to act as a visual counterbalance.

A long passage with awkward spaces and arches connected all the rooms in the flat. To disguise the irregularity and soften the angles, I papered the walls in a bold Chinese-style geometric design which I had printed specially.

This first commission was a happy experience and my sympathy with the client convinced me of the need to work as an interpreter of ideas, a principle to which I have adhered ever since. It was also a stroke of luck. My client knew people like Douglas Fairbanks Jr, Earl Beatty and the Earls of Hardwicke and Bessborough. She recommended my services and the work began to snowball. Soon I had to buy an up-to-date copy of Debrett.

At the same time, I was recommended by a friend to the General Trading Company, who were looking for someone to redesign their glass and china showroom. Public and private work began in parallel and continued that way throughout my career. Within five years I designed the first of many restaurants.

As all this illustrates, word-of-mouth plays a big part in establishing oneself as an interior designer, together with more direct publicity in magazines and newspapers. At the beginning you must grasp at any opportunity to execute a substantial job, one that can advertise your talents and provide an adequate showcase for your ideas.

Today I am in the fortunate position of having clients approach me. Since most have seen my work, either at first-hand or reproduced in my books or magazine articles, there is an element of 'pre-selection', especially in the case of public commissions. But publicity does not guarantee that potential clients will always be informed or sympathetic.

A few approach me simply because they have heard my name, and here the first steps are to show them examples of my work and establish whether or not we can work fruitfully together. Then there are others who want a room 'exactly like the one on page 132', which I designed for someone else. In such cases, I explain that it would be unfair to duplicate: the first client would no longer have an original scheme and they might end up with a look that is totally inappropriate for their needs and tastes.

During my career I have worked with many well-known people, which has generated its own kind of exposure. I designed a pair of spectacular curtains in white pillow-ticking for Lady Antonia Fraser when she was first married, and decorated Vidal Sassoon's flat before he became a household name. I remodelled Helena Rubinstein's two-storey London apartment, and decorated the home of Sir Francis and Lady Cook in the Channel Islands. Jackie Onassis ordered my carpeting for her country house; much later I had the opportunity to order one of my geometric carpet designs for HRH the Prince of Wales. After I had decorated a suite at Windsor for HRH Princess Anne, I decorated Gatcombe Park. More recently, I have completed a yacht for HM the King of Saudi Arabia and am now working on guest palaces for HM the Sultan of Oman. But however famous a client may be and however much interest and attention such an association may bring, the working relationship must still be established on an individual, private basis. The emphasis remains on uncovering each person's requirements in terms of style and practicality.

THE BRIEF

The first discussions with a client, when the scope and nature of the job are determined, are collectively known as the 'brief'. These conversations, often informal but always direct, establish many obvious parameters, such as the type of activities that must be catered for, the number of people in the household, the extent of the changes that have been planned. A good brief must also touch on more tangible aspects, such as the clients' likes and dislikes and their personal style.

Getting a proper brief from the client is one of the most important parts of the interior designer's job. Never underestimate its value. A thorough discussion of *all* the client's requirements at the outset will save much time and money later on. If you are undertaking the design of your own home, this stage is just as crucial. As I mentioned earlier, it is a good idea to enlist a partner or close friend to help you construct your own brief. Ask them to 'interview' you about your needs so you do not overlook anything; discuss your ideas in order to refine your approach.

Whether or not the client has fixed ideas about what they want, the first priority is to set practical limits to avoid wasting time by making suggestions that would be entirely unsuitable. For instance, there is no point making an electrical plan which includes picture-light wall points if the client has no pictures worth lighting. Many of the questions you ask may seem blindingly obvious or over-simple, but you would be surprised how easy it is to miss an important requirement. Some of the topics one might cover include:

*Other members of the household, including children and elderly relatives; their hobbies and activities
*The type of entertaining the client wishes to do – dinner parties, buffets, parties in the garden – and how many guests are usually asked
*How much maintenance they are prepared to undertake – do they need a home that is easy to clean and care for, or do they have help in the house?
*Do they like plants – are they active gardeners?
*Are there any pets? (I once had a London client who wanted a beehive on her terrace!)
*The type of possessions the client already owns – antiques, collections which need to be displayed, paintings, memorabilia
*The demands for storage – for clothes and personal effects, kitchen equipment, books and records
*Special activities – hobbies, work at home, television
*The nature of the property – leasehold or freehold, second home, family house or *pied-à-terre*.

And so on. If this preliminary discussion takes place in the client's home, you will have the opportunity to take a good look at what already exists. Note the general style and architectural character – are there fine features which could be emphasized or awkward corners crying out for disguise? Assess the aspect of the rooms, the views, both internal and external, and the amount of daylight each room receives. Investigate the overall layout of the space, the means of access and the flow of circulation. Houses will tell you a great deal about their owners, but do not hesitate to ask more directly about their likes and dislikes, their colour preferences and whether or not they have a fondness for a particular style or period.

Once all the practicalities have been aired and the clients have revealed something of their own tastes, my next question is always: 'What have *you* thought of doing?' This startles some people, particularly those who want to be told what to do, but it ensures that the relationship remains a two-sided one. Most people have some idea how they want their home to look, and the designer's role is to refine this approach and devise a solution that is fresh and original.

Quite often, a client will have thought of a range of ideas, all valid in themselves, which would be overwhelming, contradictory or simply impractical all in one scheme. Here the designer edits the alternatives and assesses which option has the most potential. It may be necessary to

Right My brief from the International Wool Secretariat for their offices in Carlton Gardens, London, was to create a warm and cheerful atmosphere which was nevertheless serious and business-like. Earth tones on the principal surfaces are accentuated by vivid scarlet upholstery.

point out, for example, that covering dining chairs in white is unlikely to be a good idea if there are children in the family; or to suggest that the client may soon tire of a solution already over-used. In some cases they may have to be steered away from an idea that is gimmicky or eccentric.

Of course, some people do not know what they want at all. If this is so, I develop my own ideas and watch to see how they are received. With luck, my enthusiasm is reciprocated. Once a few suggestions have been made, clients usually feel able to express an opinion and make their own contribution to help the scheme progress.

I approach every new job with great excitement. At this stage in my career, I can redesign an area mentally on first sight, and can usually judge whether the client is the kind of person who will appreciate a certain style. But while clients look to designers to be decisive on their behalf, to give direction where it is needed and express definite opinions, it is always important to bear in mind that it is the clients' home and they will have to live there.

When the job is a commercial commission, the main difference is one of scale. This does not just mean the size of the area to be considered but that the scope of the project is likely to be more encompassing. Because of this, a good brief assumes even more importance. Details must be precise and all the functional aspects thoroughly considered.

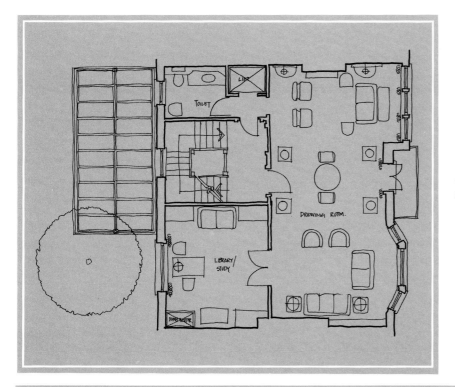

Left and below   First- and ground-floor
plans for a London house.

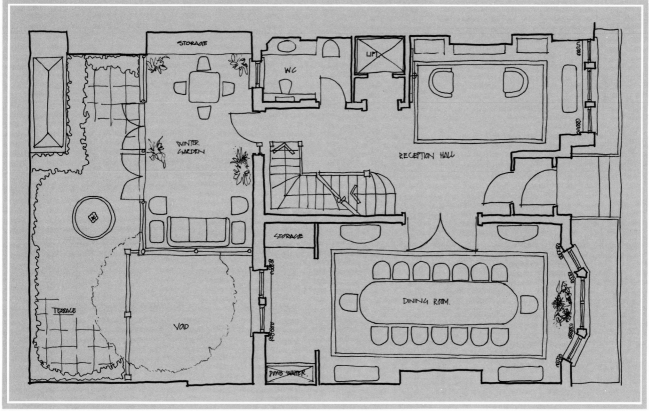

Far right Elevations of a double-height living room in Cambridge, Massachusetts. The design challenge here was how to adjust the scale of the room to make it livable without losing its drama. I suggested two abstract landscapes be hung one above the other over the Knole sofa which faces the fireplace. To the left, an unwanted view was hidden by a screen of heroic proportions, balanced on the other side by a similar one. The slight Gothic flavour introduced by the existing chimneypiece was emphasized by the ornate mirror.

The nature of the brief will depend on what is being designed. In the case of an hotel, for example, you will need to know the category, number and size of rooms, full specifications for restaurants, bars and common areas, as well as details such as the house style, symbol or logo. In office design, planning is of vital importance, to see that maximum advantage is taken of the available, often extremely expensive, space and to ensure the most efficient operation of the company. The challenge, in all cases, is to create style and atmosphere within commercial parameters.

Since most commercial clients approach designers in order to avoid the dull, ill-considered look of many public buildings, there is considerable freedom for the imagination. The proviso is that the area must work as it should – be attractive to customers, efficient to work in, or reflect the image the company is trying to promote. To achieve these aims, the brief is often necessarily very complicated and more work is usually done at this point than at any other.

DEVISING A SCHEME

After a thorough briefing, the next stage is to work out a solution to the design problem with which you have been presented. You may arrive at this quickly and intuitively – and the more experienced you are and the better acquainted with all the variables, the more this is likely to be the case.

Often, however, it is useful to spend a period in research. A scheme must be founded on a knowledge of what is actually available, the properties and uses of different materials and the degree of workmanship you can expect. If you are designing your own home, you should have already spent time familiarizing yourself with manufacturers' ranges and so on but, if not, you should certainly do so now. Go window shopping, browse through showrooms, collect catalogues and consult current magazines to ensure that what you are planning to do will be practically possible. Don't get as far as devising a scheme only to find you have based it around products that are not available.

Almost all design begins in black and white. Once you have planned the scheme on paper, you can go on to apply the colour. Sketching is an invaluable way of thinking visually, particularly if there is a difficult layout problem. To be of any use, sketches must be reasonably accurate representations of the dimensions and scale of an area, based on a detailed survey. There is no point drawing up a bathroom layout only to find that in reality the space is not wide enough to fit in the vanity unit you had planned.

Formal drawings play an important part in this process of refinement. By examining a scale plan of the area to be redesigned, one can see at a glance how to reallocate space. If structural changes are necessary, you will have to consult an architect. Architects can not only help you to execute your ideas, they can also advise on building

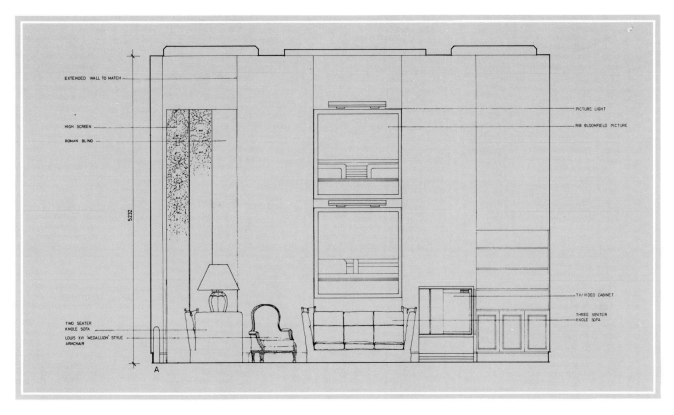

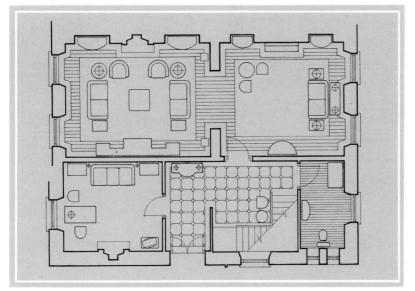

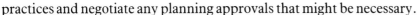

practices and negotiate any planning approvals that might be necessary.

Even if structural changes are not called for, scale plans are important tools for determining furniture and lighting layouts. In office design, these will necessarily be very detailed, particularly if the area is open plan and must be able to accommodate changes at a later date. To help you experiment with furniture arrangements you can cut to scale the shapes of sofas, chairs and tables out of brown paper and move the pieces about on the drawing.

Elevations – that is, scale drawings of the vertical elements – are also useful. They enable designers to adjust the proportions of pelmets, site pictures, wall lights and mirrors and to judge the positioning of architectural details such as cornices, chair rails and skirting boards.

Remember that services such as electricity, heating, air conditioning and plumbing will also affect what you can do. Services are inadequate or poorly planned in many houses: if the brief and the budget allow, it is advisable to consider improving any awkward arrangements. Plumbing can be particularly inhibiting. Few builders or plumbers will site a lavatory in the corner of the room with the pipe emerging diagonally, although this can sometimes improve the bathroom layout.

Similarly, the success of many schemes may depend on altering the wiring. Never underestimate the number of electrical sockets needed in a particular area. Adaptable, if slightly extravagant, wiring schemes can prevent trailing flexes ruining the appearance of a room and save a lot of money later if the layout is eventually altered.

New heating or air conditioning must be planned not only with regard to efficiency of use but also with an eye to the position of outlets such as grilles, ducts and radiators. Where such services are already installed, your options will be limited to concealment or acceptance of the existing arrangement.

Far left Public work often offers the scope for creating entirely new spaces. For this entrance hall in a prestigious office building in Piccadilly, I completely revised the internal architecture. The floor is a geometric design in travertine and black and white marble.

Above A ground-floor layout of a country house.

Aside from these everyday services, the demand is increasing for designers to be conversant with a whole range of devices, from door-opening systems and entryphones to gate control and even electronic fresh-water window washers for beachside houses. In these highly technical areas, consultations with experts are required, but the designer should advise on positioning.

Coming up with a design solution is essentially a juggling act, balancing the overall concept with the details of how it will all work. Most amateurs find it difficult to envisage a total scheme and get a sense of flow from room to room. Here it is useful to prepare a 'scheme board', a large, single sheet of card, showing the wall treatment, fabrics, carpets and colours to be used in each room throughout the house. Assembling such a panel makes it easy to see at a glance how all the elements will work together and gives you the opportunity to think about details such as the junctions between different types of floor covering and how these will be treated.

Inspiration for a scheme may come from a variety of sources. The country where an hotel is located can provide a definite starting point for the internal architecture, fabrics, colour schemes and furniture. For public spaces, a theme might inspire the decoration. In the case of a London hotel named after a famous fictional character of the nineteenth century, I developed the interior around aspects of that period, and the result has great atmosphere, with the carpet motif, typography and artefacts all displaying a Victorian flavour. Some years ago I designed a restaurant in Chelsea based on a blue and white theme, with blue and white fabrics and willow-patterned plates hung on the wall in large geometric arrangements. For a nightclub I devised a library theme; for another restaurant in Covent Garden I used the basic components of a flower market: wooden crates, a metal staircase, rough boarding and raw brick. The success of such a concept depends on extending the look to graphics such as menus, writing paper, illuminated signs, uniform insignia, linen and matchboxes.

In private work, the scheme may arise out of something the client already owns and wishes to retain in the new interior. A patterned rug, for example, may suggest a colour that could be used on the walls; a collection of watercolours may demand a subtle scheme that would not overwhelm or compete with them. Where only part of the house is being redecorated, it is essential to ensure that the new decoration works happily with the old, and your colour options may be restricted accordingly.

When a scheme is finalized, the scheme board and furniture and lighting layouts can be presented to the client. For commercial commissions, perspective drawings are also useful and save the need for complex explanations, but in the case of private work it is often best to talk the scheme through. I believe that it is disastrous to show alternatives: one scheme, well considered and based on a sound brief, is all that is necessary. If you feel the need to come up with a variety of different solutions, you have not gone through the briefing stage properly, and the client may begin to lose confidence in your judgement. This does not mean that a scheme is not open to modification. A client may well suggest some changes to the colours or dislike a particular pattern, but if you have done your job well, alterations should in general be relatively minor.

COSTING

An important determining factor in the design process is, of course, the budget. It cannot be stressed too much, however, that a successful interior is not dependent on having a vast amount of money to spend. It is dangerous to generalize, but I have found that it is often those with the most meagre budgets who are also the most amenable to new ideas and have the surest sense of their own style – perhaps because they are accustomed to the discipline of choosing between alternatives. On the whole, people who are very well off haven't taste and *nouveaux riches* need a lot of disciplining – although as one wit said not too long ago, 'better "*nouveaux*" than *never* "*riches*" '!

Below A small apartment in London is given life and style by hanging two over-scaled paintings side by side and combining elegant swan-handled chairs with more contemporary furniture.

However large or small a budget may be, the designer must work within its limits. Clients rarely set a figure they would like to spend at the initial briefing; after all, few people would venture into an antique shop, declare how much they had in their pockets and ask the dealer what this would buy them. Most clients have a rough notion of the sort of sum that is likely to be involved; it is up to the designer to set precise figures for the proposed scheme and present an estimate at the same time as the design. If the cost is way out of line with the clients' expectations, there may have to be a radical rethinking; more usually, if the budget is running a little over, a slight modification may be all that is needed.

An alternative to the single, fixed budget is to spread the cost of the work over a period of time, say five to seven years. The work can be done in stages – for example, a room a year – and paid for in instalments. In practice, most people who do not use professional designers operate in this way and, aside from the financial advantages, there is a lot to be said for developing an interior gradually through a natural progression rather than making a sudden transformation.

If you are not relying on an interior designer to work out a detailed estimate, you will have to undertake this yourself, but it is important to realize that the whole question of budgeting is not simply a case of adding up all the figures quoted by the various suppliers and then seeing whether or not you can afford the total. As in every area of design, budgeting demands the ability to make appropriate choices. Money must be spent where it will make the most effective contribution to the whole interior. Enough must be set aside for sound preparation of surfaces, good fittings such as door furniture, switches and sockets and all the other details that contribute so much to a room. In such a setting, ordinary objects look better, whereas a lavish focal point in a shoddy environment only accentuates the contrast.

When the budget is limited, allocating resources calls for ingenuity and imagination. Most people fail to realize that luxury is not synonymous with spending a fortune. Fine materials such as silk, velvet, marble and ebony, good antiques, pictures and high-quality craftsmanship *are* expensive, but to achieve something of the same quality with limited funds the answer is not to opt for a cheap simulation or reproduction, which will always look second-rate, but to adopt radically different solutions.

I am often challenged by working to a small budget, whether the job is a small apartment for a newly married couple, a temporary room setting for a charity, a hotel where a simple refurbishment is required or a showroom, which must be frequently changed and hence economical. Many years ago, when Vidal Sassoon was not even on the first rung of the ladder to the top, I decorated a tiny apartment in Curzon Place for him and his wife. Over bookshelves on which all the paperbacks were covered with white cartridge paper, I hung curtains made of simple

Far left The splendid atrium in a private house in Athens. The small Henry Moore group has now been replaced by a much larger one more in scale with the space.

chair lining. Two Victorian chairs in the style of Louis XV were repainted beige and upholstered in white leather. The total cost was only £500, but the effect was elegant and stylish. When my French associate wanted the walls in our Paris showroom to look as though they were covered in parchment, he stuck six-inch-square pieces of off-white cartridge paper to the walls, gluing only the centre of each square for a slightly *tremblant* and magical look. In my first old-rose garden in Suffolk, I couldn't afford *treillage* obelisks for rambling roses, so I bought four cheap aluminium saucepan stands and painted them beige. These examples concern details, but display the degree of cost-effectiveness and ingenuity that can be extended to an entire scheme.

RUNNING A JOB

After the scheme has been approved by the client, the next stage is the execution. It is up to the designer to ensure that work proceeds smoothly, running to schedule and to budget. In this capacity, the designer's role is to draw up an efficient timetable for the job, coordinate the services of sub-contractors, tradesmen and suppliers, and supervise the quality of workmanship. This means, for example, ordering any imported fabrics well in advance to allow for delivery time, making sure all structural work, re-wiring or re-plumbing is completed before decoration is begun and checking each stage thoroughly before it is too late to rectify mistakes.

It is in this area that many amateurs go astray. Common sense should be your guide: it is obviously a mistake to lay a new carpet before re-plastering and re-painting, or to re-plaster before new wiring is installed. Take the time before you commission the work to check with sub-contractors and suppliers about their requirements and the time they estimate it will take to do the job. At this point, ensure that you have received a full specification for the work as part of the cost estimate. Unless everything is set down very clearly on paper you may find yourself charged for extra items as the work progresses. A carpenter engaged to hang new doors, for example, may bill you for new hinges if these were not mentioned in the original estimate. Small amounts like this can add up alarmingly. Once all the details have been sorted out, draw up a schedule of work so that no one stage holds up the next. And be prepared to spend a good deal of time overseeing the actual work.

Many problems can be side-stepped by making sure that you use reliable firms in the first place. Ask around for recommendations and take up references if necessary. I always use first class sub-contractors, whose work I know and respect.

A recent London commission of mine provides a good illustration of the progress of a typical job. I was asked to look at a two-storey apartment, where the clients wanted to enlarge the main reception area and incorporate the roof garden by turning it into a conservatory cum dining room. The clients had their own architect and he and I discussed all the various problems and solutions during the briefing.

To make a more generous entrance hall, and a passage with more architectural character, we decided to re-position the hall cupboards and exaggerate the proportions of the existing area by building shallow vaulting and installing a large section of mirror in a wide alcove. These changes added a great sense of space and made the area more interesting.

Upstairs, we agreed to treat the new glazed addition in a different manner to the old living room, but to make the opening between the two as wide as was structurally possible. In the existing living room we knew that the mundane and badly proportioned sheet-glass windows should be re-made to match the glazing in the new area. We also felt that the 1960s fireplace was inadequate, as were the cornice, architraves and skirting. I found an attractive Regency stone surround for the fireplace, and together we devised a Soane-esque cornice, jibbed two doors and re-drew the skirting. I asked for the second chimney breast to be lost by fitting a recess with flush cupboards. The planning stage was protracted by the need to obtain official approval for the structural changes from the head landlord and the local authority.

While all this was underway, my assistant and I decided which antique furniture was to be used, temporarily hung the pictures, to make sure they were correctly positioned before the electrician installed picture-light points, and ordered the carpet after colour trials had been approved for the specified design. The carpet had a geometric pattern flanked by a lined border which followed the contour of the living room. It also extended down the stairs and along the entrance hall but, to maintain the sense of space, we only used the border in the large upstairs area.

Paint and fabric colours were coordinated with the carpet colour-way. Although the bedrooms and study were not part of the original brief, great attention was paid to considering how the new colour scheme would work with these connecting areas. Green, yellow and off-white were chosen for the entrance and reception areas, which meet the pale blue of the main bedroom very happily.

In this particular job, with its elements of design and decoration, the demand for proper coordination and consultation were high. The design not only had to meet with the clients' approval, but had to be drawn up in conjunction with their architect and passed by the landlord and planning department. The decoration also had to work harmoniously with the other areas of the apartment which were outside the brief. With so many factors involved, rigorous organization and attention to detail were of paramount importance.

SPECIAL COMMISSIONS

If the client requires new furniture, objects or pictures, as well as a new decorative scheme, part of the designer's job is to act as a supplier. This can entail literally embarking on shopping expeditions with the client, or producing a design of your own which will be made up to order. Many jobs present the opportunity to create a new pattern for fabric, wallpaper or carpet, design a table or pair of chairs or commission an original painting. In fact, this may be the only way to achieve the precise look you and the client want.

I have always welcomed such challenges and, over the years, what began as single commissions have developed into a flourishing business. I devised my first patterned carpet in 1960 and today over two hundred are in production, available through my company or the various firms who make them. Even if you do not intend to launch an entire range, creating your own design can be extremely satisfying. Many manufacturers are willing to make up 'one-off' designs but bear in mind that economies of scale make this an expensive option. Similarly, it is possible to work closely with craftsmen to have special pieces of

Right A dining room in a London flat presents a dramatic use of light. The glass-topped column table, based on one of my designs, seems suspended over the dining chairs – a theatrical touch particularly appropriate in a dining room or restaurant.

furniture made to your own specifications. As always, research is an important part of the process. Discover the companies or individuals who produce the sort of item you are looking for, ask to see examples of their previous work, investigate the range of materials thoroughly and oversee the production to ensure your design is executed properly.

Commissioning an original painting, print or piece of sculpture can add an exciting dimension to any scheme. Although this practice may sound unusual today, it is really no more than a version of the time-honoured system of patronage. An interior designer can keep abreast of new talent and recommend an artist for a client just as he would advise on a furniture maker. By briefing an artist on scale, mood and colour, the designer can ensure that the result will enhance its setting. In 1958, for Vidal Sassoon's Bond Street salon, I commissioned Dennis Wirth-Miller to create an abstract painting, which introduced a striking element to the reception area. More recently, I have interviewed artists for a client in Cambridge, Massachusetts, who had previously lacked the time to collect pictures for herself.

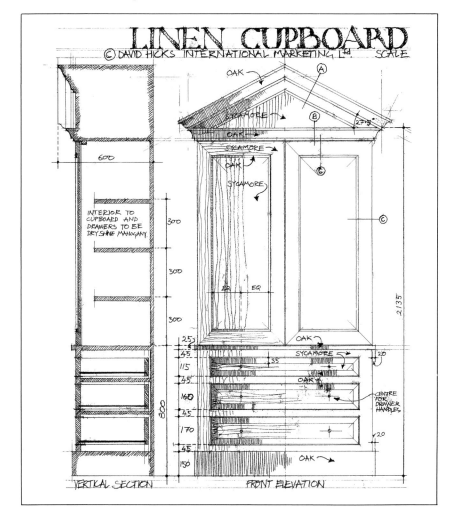

Left Designs for furniture such as this linen cupboard may start out as a special commission for a particular client and then become incorporated into our range if they proved popular and successful.

CHAPTER TWO

THE DESIGNER'S PALETTE

The previous chapter stressed the need for the designer to be technically proficient, well-informed about materials and their uses, capable of interpreting clients' wishes in a practical, sympathetic manner and of executing a scheme in collaboration with other specialists. This chapter will deal with more aesthetic issues – the raw materials of colour, texture, pattern and form, which together make up the designer's palette.

These basic elements could – and, for the serious designer, should – become a lifelong preoccupation. I have noticed that there is a touchstone, a certain consistency, that can be discerned in the work of many great designers, past and present. It is not as defined as a set of rules, nor as nebulous as instinct, but is the process whereby different individuals, via different routes, come to much the same conclusions about design. This does not mean that their work looks the same, but that the same basic principles can be detected beneath it all.

Here it is important to say that rules are meant to be broken. Many of the most successful schemes derive their impact from a startling combination of colours or a novel conjunction of patterns which fly in the face of accepted practice. Rules give structure, but often at the expense of vitality.

The designer should not only recognize the importance of certain fundamental principles, but also be prepared to bend or even break rules creatively.

In this chapter we examine colour, texture, pattern and form separately, in order to concentrate on their unique characteristics and assess the special contribution each one can make to the interior. You may well admire a sofa for its colour, a rug for its texture, a fabric for its pattern or a vase for its shape, but in reality such things are interdependent. Colour will vary according to texture and according to the other colours to which it is adjacent; pattern joins textures and shapes and colours in a rhythmic arrangement; form, proportion and shape define how it is all perceived. When it comes to practical applications, you must be able to work with all these elements at the same time.

COLOUR

No one aspect of interior design has acquired so many rules and inspired so much deliberation as colour. From the technical complexities of colour theory and the exhaustive colour charts of paint manufacturers to homespun nursery proverbs, there is plentiful evidence of our attempts to organize and understand the subject.

This is not surprising. Colour is the single most powerful component of any interior. It can make the maximum change to any area – even more than lighting. It can transform ordinary space into one filled with atmosphere; wrongly applied, it can deprive a magnificent period room of all its charm and interest. Of the many raw materials at the designer's disposal colour is the most exciting and rewarding – and the most dangerous.

Most people, understandably, are afraid of colour. Because of this they rely on rules to tell them which colour goes with which other, and they generally opt for safe, dull schemes that can't go wrong, but lack flair and imagination.

The remedy, I believe, is not to study colour theory or copy, down to the last tint, a colour scheme devised by someone else. It is to spend time going back to basics, becoming acquainted with colour as it is used all around you. Like food, colour is to be enjoyed. It works on a visceral level, and only by broadening your experience can you begin to assess the impact of a particular shade or the effectiveness of a certain combination.

Sources

Nature is the starting point for our colour awareness. The moods we attribute to different colours reflect these primitive associations: blue is cold, like ice, red is warm, like fire, green is as soothing as a field, yellow is cheerful, like sunlight. A step further and natural landscapes provide much inspiration: the subtle greys, mauves and purples of a heather-clad moor, the outrageous vibrant reds of a North American woodland in autumn, the exquisite freshness of an Alpine meadow dotted with wildflowers.

Although nature never gets it wrong, when it is tamed and cultivated in the garden or hothouse the results are sometimes less than fortunate. Our ability to breed species well beyond their natural state has given us the freedom to make mistakes. Yet the finest gardens and man-made landscapes still provide a rich source of colour ideas. Old-rose gardens can teach you how to combine different shades of red and pink; woodland planting shows a subtle interplay of greens; even a lichened garden wall will reveal a tapestry of different tones if you look closely.

Art – particularly the works of the great masters of colour – is always stimulating. When I go to an exhibition or museum I often make notes of colour combinations that I think will be useful at some point. Look at paintings by the French artist Marie Laurencin for pinks, blues and apple greens; at Picasso's early period for blues and pinks; at the ability of Odilon Redon to combine red poppies with blue cornflowers. Van Gogh suggested the heat of Provence in his use of yellows and browns, while the Japanese artist Foujita can teach you a great deal about the power of monochrome and the different shades of white.

Art also gives us an accurate picture of how colour was used in the past. In the early eighteenth century, rich, dark colours were fashionable – spinach greens, mulberry reds and searing Chinese yellows. Towards the end of the century, clear pastel colours were popular, together with a great deal of white. Then, during the Regency period, dark colours made a comeback, but enlivened with brilliant lemon yellows, peacock blues and raspberry pinks. We can be confident in our knowledge of these changing colour fashions because of the existence of many contemporary references, including the magnificent Adam folios in the Soane Museum in London and the Directoire drawings in the Louvre.

During the Victorian age, colours were sombre; not the depressing palette many people imagine, but a rich and subtle combination of tones such as chestnut brown, purple and indigo. Pale yellows, creams, pinks and greys came into fashion with the Edwardinans, to be overthrown by the garish discord of orange, mauve and jade green in the 1920s. The antidote to this was Syrie Maugham's off-white interiors of the 1930s, perhaps the first 'modern' colour look in interior design.

Aside from art and historical sources, other aspects of culture can attune the designer to the use of colour. Because they are so exaggerated, costume and set designs for ballet, opera and the theatre can suggest a new approach. The cinema can also be inspiring, as can photography, book illustrations, advertisements and even greetings cards and packaging. Fashion designers such as Givenchy, Saint Laurent and Quant have stimulated many of my colour ideas. Travel – even the armchair variety – can also broaden your appreciation of colour: look at Indian and Central American cultures for brilliant, vibrant combinations.

I have enjoyed experimenting with colour all my life. I never learned colour theory and believe categorizing certain combinations as 'discordant' or 'complementary' can be misleading and inhibiting. To me, pink and red, for example, do not 'clash', they 'vibrate', in a stimulating and interesting way. I did, however, learn much from other people. During my early career, Mrs Benson and Lady Bessborough taught me not to try to cram too much colour into an interior, and my friends Roderick Cameron and Winnie Portarlington taught me most of what I know about arranging objects united by colour. I have also been influenced by the work of John Fowler, who founded the celebrated interior design firm of Colefax and Fowler. Perhaps the greatest colourist of the century, he would spend days mixing and dyeing to achieve the precise shades he wanted.

Combining colours

There are really very few colours that do not go together, if you use the right shade of each. Much will depend on experiment. The slightest variation in the amount of blue in a pink, for example, will determine whether or not it will go with a certain bluish brown. Invest some time mixing colours and putting various shades together – a set of artist's pastel colours or gouache is ideal for the purpose and will increase both your skill and your confidence. But bear in mind that paint colours do not tell the whole story. Colours change according to the reflectivity or texture of the surface – the same shade of blue will look different in silk or in a cut-pile wool carpet, in matt paint or in a lacquer finish. Lighting also has an effect; ensure that you view colour swatches by electric (never fluorescent) light and at different times of the day.

The simplest way to use colours in an interior is not to combine them at all, but to coordinate different shades of the same colour – a room decorated entirely in different greens, for example, can be very successful. All variations of a colour work together: all reds, blues, greens, yellows, browns, greys and so on. Coordination is both easy to achieve and sophisticated in effect – in fact, it is an almost foolproof way for many people to produce an attractive decorative scheme.

More interesting combinations arise from using families of near shades, such as reds and pinks, blues and greens, yellows, oranges and browns and the natural or neutral shades of white, beige, grey and

Right This bedroom in a Portuguese villa shows the potential of decorating entirely in white. This treatment emphasizes the textural quality of different surfaces.

Far right The Duke and Duchess of Abercorn's entrance hall in Northern Ireland has elaborate plasterwork by William Vitruvius Morrison, picked out in two shades of melon to reflect some of the subtle colours of the oriental rug. A ping-pong table usually stands here and the hall is as much in use as any other room in the house.

Far left The view from the drawing room of my country house through to the hall, with its yellow stippled wallpaper. The paper is banded with a chocolate-coloured paper. A scrubbed-stone floor runs the length of the house. The balustrade design is based on a late-eighteenth-century example.

Left and below Hosta seiboldiana and artichokes nestle in a porphyrised cache-pot set beside jade and porcelain vases, complementing the eau-de-nil walls – an example of effective colour coordination that even extends to flower arrangements.

black. Here the proportion of each colour makes a difference. In a simple example, an arrangement of twelve cream roses, six deep yellow and three orange-coloured ones is far more effective than using equal amounts of the three different shades. But keep the colours together.

The most vital colour schemes, however, require more expertise. The secret is to select a basic palette of related colours and then build up a collection of contrasts and accents to bring it all to life. Translated into an interior, the principle works by allocating the basic palette colours to the carpet, walls and curtains and injecting interesting contrasts in the form of accessories and smaller items of furniture. For example, in a room mostly decorated in beige, brown and white, I would add 'vibrating' pink and yellow silk cushions.

Certain combinations just won't work. I personally detest orange and peacock blue, and orange and mid-green. Pink and magenta work with green but not with blue. Other combinations of strong colours such as scarlet and midnight blue may be too overpowering for a private house, even though they look wonderful together. Unexpectedly successful combinations, on the other hand, include light blue with mink brown, beige with pale shell pink or pale mauve, yellow with many pinks (but not red).

Helena Rubinstein's north-facing London drawing room displayed one of the most dramatic and daring colour schemes I have ever assembled. When I asked Madame what colour she had in mind for the walls, she simply snipped a strip of purple silk from the hem of her Balenciaga dress and asked me to have tweed woven to the same shade. Pinks, scarlets and magentas were chosen for the upholstery and soft furnishing and, to tie it all together, I commissioned textured rugs in dark aubergine.

Using colour

Unless the internal architecture is absolutely perfect in every detail – which is as difficult to live with as it is to achieve – then colour is a vital ingredient in the interior. Colour preferences are highly personal, so the first task of the designer is to establish whether the client has an aversion to any particular one or a fondness for another. But choosing colour for a decorative scheme involves questions of context as well as taste. The issues to consider include:

*The location of the house or apartment: town or country; whether or not there is a garden; climate and nature of surrounding landscape
*Aspect: the orientation of the property; the degree and quality of natural light each room receives
*Function and uses of the rooms: from practical requirements to the atmosphere you wish to create
*The colours of any existing features or possessions which are being retained.

Far left Using colour successfully in the interior demands great flair. In my Paris showroom, blue-pink walls and the viridian green of the sofa reflect the pink and green of the superb eighteenth-century architectural plans hung on the wall. A shocking pink blanket draws the two shades together. Marblized tole columns hold Louis XVI porphyry gilt-mounted vases. The fauteuil was designed by my French associate, Christian Badin.

Some colour schemes

SCHEME	WALLS	CURTAINS	CARPET
Beige	Pale beige	Pale beige	Dark brown
	Mid-beige	White	Mid-beige
	White	Beige and white	Pale beige
	Deep beige	Chocolate brown	White
Brown	Coca-Cola	Chestnut brown	Black and brown
	Milk chocolate	String	Dark brown
	White	Chestnut	Dark brown
	Cinnamon brown	String	Orange
Red	Maroon	Scarlet	Aubergine
	Scarlet	Red and white	Maroon
	White	Scarlet	White
	String	Saffron yellow	Chocolate brown
White	Pale string	Pale string	White
	Pale grey	White	Pale string
	White	White	White
	White	White and sand	White textured
Blue	Pale aquamarine	White	Moss green
	Slate blue	Yellow	Gold
	White	Turquoise	Khaki
	String	Cornflower blue	White
Yellow	White	Yellow	Milk chocolate
	Chinese yellow	Tobacco	Bronze green
	Faded coral	Saffron yellow	Bronze green
	String	Mole brown	Chocolate brown
Green	Lettuce	Cabbage	Grass
	Cedar green	Pale blue	Cedar green
	Ice green	Ice green	Blue and green
	White	Green and white	White
Pink	Palest pink	White	Sand
	White	Pale pink	Scarlet
	Beige	Raspberry	Chocolate brown
	Shocking pink	Periwinkle blue	Chestnut brown
Grey	Pearl grey	White	Yellow
	White	Grey	Black and white
	Pink grey	Dark brown	White
	Dark	Light	Black

All these schemes are in very definite colour ranges and it is possible to intermix them to a certain degree. The texture plays an important part and so does the exact shade of a colour.

SOFA	CHAIRS	CUSHIONS	FLOWERS
Milk chocolate	Chinese yellow	White	Orange
Chestnut brown	Black	Deep orange	Yellow
Brown and white	Chocolate brown	Vermilion	White
Black	Chestnut brown	Cream	Pale pink
White	Natural	Scarlet	Shocking pink
Black and brown	Coral red	Turquoise	White
String	Dark brown	Dark brown	Scarlet
Black	Yellow	Cinnamon brown	Pink
Vermilion	Cherry red	Shocking pink	Scarlet
White	Magenta	Scarlet	Pink
Scarlet	Maroon	Pink	Pink
Coral red	White	Shocking pink	Scarlet
Honey	Silver grey	White	White
White	White	Lemon	White
Black and white	Black	Black	Brilliant yellow
Natural	White	Natural	Mixed
Turquoise	Blue and green	Saffron yellow	Green leaves
Cedar green	Blue	Daffodil yellow	Blue
Lettuce	Emerald	Turquoise	Pink
Blue and white	Cornflower blue	Pale cerulean	Blue
Orange and white	Yellow	Deep shocking pink	Orange
White	Orange and green	Orange	Coral
Brilliant orange	Chocolate brown	Shocking pink	Flame
Saffron yellow	Orange	Tangerine	Mauve
Emerald	Turquoise	Lime	White and yellow
Green and white	Black	Turquoise	Mauve and purple
Olive	Grass green	White	White
Khaki	White	Emerald	Yellow
Moss green	Scarlet	Shocking pink	Scarlet
Red and white	Cornflower blue	Scarlet	Yellow
Scarlet	Orange	Lemon	Shocking pink
Scarlet	Coral	Tangerine	Scarlet
Dark grey	Black	Lemon	Yellow
Dark grey	Grey and black	String	White
Black	Dark grey	Black and white	Yellow
Black and white	Scarlet	Scarlet	Scarlet

Colours should be appropriate to the country and climate: northern Europe demands a different palette from the Mediterreanean, and certain colours work better in an urban setting, others in the countryside.

Colour can also go a long way to remedy the disadvantages of a particular location. Soft pinks or rich earth colours will warm up a chilly north-facing room; a fresh pastel will alleviate the gloom of a semi-basement; a smart grey will introduce elegance to a city apartment. But it is as well to be aware of what colour cannot do. Despite its power, it is not a panacea for whatever ails your interior. It cannot cover up a poor structure or disguise a bad surface and, contrary to popular belief, it has little impact on the basic proportions of a room. You can't visually lower a high ceiling by painting it a dark colour; painting a ceiling white will not increase the impression of height.

Ultimately, the functions of the various rooms will provide the strongest directives for a colour scheme. Although the scope remains wide, certain types of colours suit different rooms and will enhance the uses to which they are put.

Entrances, stairs and passageways – the backbone of the house – are often best given a neutral treatment. This is because they act as connecting areas between rooms which may need quite different colour schemes. A vivid treatment in a hall would simply limit your options in every room leading off it. If a passageway is rambling and awkwardly shaped, a positive colour scheme may lend interest and coherence, but it will have to be carefully coordinated with the other rooms in the house to avoid unfortunate contrasts.

The living room offers greater scope for the imagination. Generally, for homes in the country or those with a garden, light, clear colours will complement any views and help give an atmosphere of freshness; the object is to make the living room an extension of its setting, not to set up an uneasy battle for attention. Homes in the city, on the other hand, can take more sophisticated colours – rich reds, set off by black lacquer-work, for example, would make a striking statement in a town drawing room.

Darker schemes are also suitable for libraries or studies, whatever their location. The richer shades create a cosy, warm background against which old book bindings or new dust jackets can glow.

Dining rooms, since they are not in constant use, can take an element of theatricality – but not so much as to detract from the intimacy of dining. Deep, dramatic colours can be used here, even in the country, but remember that not all entertaining takes place at night; the colours should not be so overpowering that the room is unsuitable for daytime use.

Traditionally, bedrooms are often given 'feminine' colour schemes. In fact, any pale, soft tones are successful. Avoid striking patterns or bright, primary colours, which are not conducive to repose. In children's rooms, however, primary colours strike a cheerful note. Here, for the sake of economy, keep the wall and floor colours fairly subdued and reserve the paintbox shades for inexpensive accessories that can be discarded as the children grow up.

Bathrooms, increasingly less neglected, can accommodate a wide variety of styles, but should be decorated to suit the room they adjoin. Pretty pastels look well in a bathroom leading off a bedroom; a downstairs cloakroom could be effectively given a masculine, tailored look. A classical black and white or neutral scheme works best if there is only one bathroom in the home.

Kitchens are rooms where people spend a good deal of time and, as well as being places where you must be able to work efficiently, should also be cheerful and welcoming. Highly dramatic or hectic colour schemes should be avoided. Fresh, clean and clear versions of almost any colour are suitable.

Because each room makes its own demands in terms of atmosphere, function and aspect, there is a danger that you may come up with a series of colour schemes that will not work together in the house as a whole. Here the solution is to plan your choice of colours using a scheme board (see page 44). This will help you edit your ideas and prevent visual indigestion. If you are only decorating part of your house, a scheme board will help you come up with a solution that blends sympathetically with existing colours.

Colour works in just the same way when you are devising a scheme for a company or a public client, but your options will be strictly defined by the nature of the job. Offices and reception areas, for example, should not be controversial – avoid highly personal colour choices. In companies with a fast turnover of staff it is best to adopt a fairly neutral scheme, with accents of colour that can easily be altered. Similarly, for showrooms and shops, the colours should be appealing, yet not detract from the merchandise on display.

The decoration of restaurants, bars and nightclubs, however, offers the designer a freer rein. Here the aim is to produce an evocative environment with the emphasis on entertainment. Since the areas are much larger than in private homes, dramatic colour combinations can be used to great effect. Some time ago, I was asked to decorate the revolving restaurant on top of the GPO (now British Telecom) Tower, one of London's modern landmarks. At 550 feet above the ground, the restaurant offered panoramic views of the city. Accordingly, the decoration had to be striking yet not distract the attention of diners. I chose midnight blue for the walls and ceiling, commissioned a carpet in the same blue, patterned with a finely drawn motif in scarlet, and hung Roman blinds, also blue and trimmed with scarlet.

There is one colour scheme that will work in almost every location, and that is no colour. Monochromatic or all-white schemes are highly effective and can be the very essence of modernity. But there are two important provisos. The first is that the whites or off-whites you use must be complementary. Whites vary subtly in tone: cool, bluish-white tiles, for example, will make richer, yellowish-white paintwork look dingy. (Of course, you can play on this and assemble different whites for curtains, carpets, furniture and accessories.) The second proviso is that all-white or neutral schemes demand a high degree of perfection, not only in terms of the interior architecture and finishes but also in terms of what is displayed. Since this treatment literally dissolves space, throwing into relief whatever the room contains, objects, pictures and furniture must be of real quality, whatever the period, to be able to stand the scrutiny.

TEXTURE

Textural variety adds a subtle yet stimulating dimension to an interior. Most homes already contain much potential – the matt surface of plasterwork, the graininess of woodwork, the smoothness of marble fireplaces and the reflective sheen of tiling. A decorative scheme should develop and extend this built-in variety.

Texture is important, because it draws us into a room by stimulating our sense of touch, heightening our perception of comfort. It also adds depth to the plainest interior by creating interesting variations of light and shade in circumstances where a forthright pattern would be obtrusive. Part of our enjoyment of texture arises from nature – think of a country walk over grass, ploughed earth, stony ground. To change the metaphor, no good chef would offer a meal consisting of minced meat, puréed vegetables and mashed potatoes. In interiors too, contrast whets the appetite.

Texture is neither a difficult nor an expensive quality to exploit, but it is often surprisingly neglected. A simple exercise is to assemble on a table objects that are all one colour but of different textures: for example, rock crystal, perspex and a glass vase holding white freesias. With colour playing a minor role, the invitation is to the sense of touch. Extended to the interior as a whole, any scheme relying on strict colour coordination should display sharp contrasts of texture to avoid being bland and uninteresting.

Fabric is an important source of texture in the home. Choose upholstery and soft furnishings with an eye to the interest of the weave as well as colour and pattern. Slub weaves are ever-popular, if a trifle over-used; even-weave, coarse pure wool makes an exciting alternative. Glazed-cotton or silk-taffeta cushions provide a good contrast to a sofa upholstered in a matt-textured fabric such as wool or coarse linen. On matt-fabric curtains I often use a glazed-chintz band on the leading edge; if the curtains are glazed chintz, I add a dull cotton fringe.

Fabric-covered walls immediately introduce a strong note of texture to a room. Plain cotton and hessian are economic alternatives – nowadays few can afford the luxury of silk damask. I have often used

Far right A tablescape all in neutral shades is composed of a contemporary Japanese painting, a white pottery lamp, a Chinese jade cup and saucer and prehistoric pottery vases, all arranged on a beige and white hessian tablecloth.

clothing fabric such as grey flannel or tweed to line the walls of an intimate room such as a bedroom or study; once I covered the walls of a dressing room in camelhair – expensive, but highly effective.

Walls can also be covered with textured wallpaper, but here it is important to be discriminating. Avoid the heavily embossed papers designed to simulate brick, stone or rough plaster – they don't look like the real thing and have been used too often in public houses by builders anxious to hide irregularities in the plasterwork. (The same advice applies to textured paint.) Flock wallpaper, with its slightly raised surface, can look very sumptuous; this was a very fashionable treatment immediately after the war.

The floor provides an opportunity to combine textures in an interesting way. Different areas of the home demand different solutions underfoot, but you can also mix different types of material in the same area: stone and terracotta tiles; area rugs on polished floorboards; coir matting on brick.

Below A bed hung with antique velvet drapery in a plain colour contrasts with the patterns elsewhere in the room. Blue is the link between the porcelain, patterned wallpaper, upholstery and rug, each of which displays a different, but complementary pattern.

Such a simple ingredient as paint should also be exploited. Paint comes in three basic finishes: matt, eggshell and gloss. Matt, or eggshell, is typically chosen for walls and ceilings, eggshell and gloss for doors and woodwork. But there is no reason why you should not reverse the procedure and set off walls or door panels that have been varnished for a lacquer-like effect with matt trim.

It is hard to go wrong with texture, unlike the more controversial areas of colour and pattern. Texture often suggests luxury, principally because the most expensive materials are often inherently interesting texurally. The same cannot be said of synthetics and, in general, it is best to avoid totally man-made materials if you can. But this does not mean that textural quality has to be expensive. The nubbliness of coir and hessian, the coarseness of old brick or flagstones, the delicacy of wickerwork can be charming, and they are all cheap.

PATTERN

Pattern can be abstract or figurative; bold, rich or muted; formal, demure or evocative. As well as introducing colour, pattern adds rhythm and life to an interior. It can also soften harsh angles, create a period atmosphere, even adjust the proportions and scale of a room.

Since time began we have surrounded ourselves with decorative patterns. There is something inherently satisfying about a repeated design, and every culture has evolved different ways of making patterns, using traditional motifs that have survived through the centuries. As well as these folk designs, which are often adapted by modern textile designers, the interior designer has access to a tremendous breadth of choice thanks to present-day techniques of mass production and marketing. Pattern has never been more accessible but, like any other element in the interior, it must be used appropriately to make the most of its potential.

Sources

The sources discussed for colour (see page 54) apply equally well to pattern. Art, history, fashion and graphic design yield abundant examples of pattern in a variety of contexts, many of which can be reinterpreted for use in the interior.

Particular inspiration can be taken from painters such as Édouard Vuillard (1868–1940) whose charming and intimate studies of interiors portray interesting combinations of patterned wallpapers and textiles. For period motifs it is worth looking at eighteenth-century conversation-piece pictures, or visiting historic collections of textiles and prints in museums such as the Victoria and Albert Museum in London. Many books also exist which contain accurate representations of wallpaper, carpet and fabric designs. I have found much inspiration in Owen Jones' *Grammar of Ornament*, first published in 1856, an invaluable record of the motifs and decorative designs of every civilization.

Visiting historic houses will also teach you how pattern was used in previous centuries. Remember, however, that many of these designs have lost their original brilliance due to fading and discoloration – some of the colours used in early printing were fugitive and may have disappeared altogether.

Folk patterns from around the world are a constant source of ideas for the designer. The designs of Persian carpets, kelims and dhurries from the Indian subcontinent, Mexican basketwork, African textiles, North American quilting and Moorish mosaics have all been borrowed at one time or another, and regularly appear transformed on furnishing fabrics, carpeting and bed-linen. For traditional interiors, there is a wide variety of patterned fabrics available, making this one of the most versatile ranges of merchandise in the world.

Patterns, like everything else, go in and out of fashion. An important breakthrough in recent years was the success of Laura Ashley in reintroducing enchanting small patterns to a wide market. Many manufacturers today follow her example and produce coordinated ranges, with the same designs available in different colour-ways or in different scales.

There is no reason, however, why you should have to rely on what is commercially available. A large commission may offer the designer the

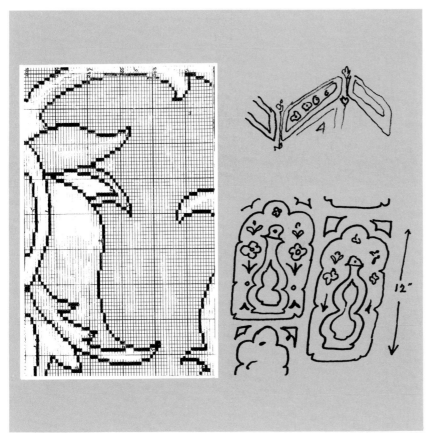

Far left My son's bedroom in France had a tester bed with a straight pelmet, hung with a geometric blue, brown and cream fabric. Sheets and towels are in a matching design and the Indian cotton carpet on the floor is in the same colours.

Left I design geometric patterns for carpets and fabrics by sketching ideas for motifs. The finished designs are then produced in my studio.

opportunity to create an original pattern for a fabric or carpet, or the chance to reprint a traditional design which is now out of production. For the amateur these options may prove too expensive to execute on a small scale, but such simple decorative techniques as stencilling will enable you to inject a fresh and personal note.

I was first provoked to design a pattern for a carpet in 1960 when I was unable to find any interesting geometric designs on the market. Over the years, some of my ideas have come from the most mundane sources – even cast-iron manhole covers – and I am currently developing designs based on Japanese heraldic motifs. My research has convinced me that there is nothing new in the field of pattern design, but there remains tremendous scope for reinterpretation.

Using pattern

Using pattern successfully really comes down to using it appropriately. In addition to colour, there is the scale of the design and the character of the motif to consider.

The colours displayed by a pattern should fit in with the overall decorative scheme. This does not necessarily mean that all the colours have to be repeated elsewhere in the room, but the general effect should complement what already exists. Of course, it can also work the other way round. A pattern may have an interesting colour combination which you can use as a ready-made foundation for a scheme.

When choosing the pattern design or motif, you should be guided by common sense. Floral and figurative prints are at home in the country and in intimate rooms such as bedrooms; abstract designs suit contemporary interiors. Formal, geometric patterns are always elegant and can blend happily with antiques in a period setting, or work equally well in the tailored environment of a company boardroom, a modern city apartment or a public space such as a hotel foyer.

The scale of the pattern – the size of the motif and the frequency of repeat – also has a part to play. A large pattern can be overwhelming if it is used in a small area; if it is used in small amounts you simply will not gain the full effect of the repeat. Smaller, almost textural, designs add interest where the space is more confined, but lose their impact in grander areas.

Most problems are generated when people attempt to combine different patterns in the same interior. There are some simple rules which you can apply in this situation: large-scale patterns will work with medium- and small-sized ones, and medium-sized patterns go with small designs, but very small patterns should not be put together with very large ones. The transition in terms of scale must not be abrupt, neither should both patterns be the same size. The patterns should also be colour-coordinated to the extent that at least one colour appears in both fabrics and should display what I call affinity in terms of design. If you follow these guidelines, it is possible to build up layer upon layer of pattern and achieve a real sense of depth. In most rooms, however, where only a couple of patterns may be used, it is important to have an equivalent amount of plain surfaces to mediate between the different designs. Patterned wallpaper often looks best with plain curtains and vice versa. Similarly, avoid using differently patterned carpets in adjoining areas.

Pattern can also be used entirely on its own – a richly detailed Oriental rug may be all the pattern you need in a room. Here the quality and interest of the design is important, because you are effectively putting the pattern on display, in the same way you would by hanging a work of art on the wall.

FORM

The appreciation of form is the designer's sixth sense. On a simple level, form concerns shapes and how they relate to one another – in other words, questions of proportion, scale and arrangement. But a real understanding depends on the ability to appreciate volume. Every good designer must be able to work in three dimensions, to assess how objects will work within the volume of a given space.

This sounds technical, but it involves no more than common-sense judgement gained through everyday experience. In practical terms, awareness of form enables the designer to choose the right size and shape of lampshade to go with a particular base, to arrange pictures on a wall, to choose furniture that suits the scale of the room, to place a chair rail at the correct height, to judge the proper depth of a skirting board. It is also what enables the designer to take decisions about spatial organization, including changes to the fabric and structure of a building.

Looking at buildings is the best way to learn about form. Make a thorough study of good examples from different periods, paying attention to the internal detailing as well as the overall architectural quality. Note how certain shapes, such as the pyramid, obelisk and column, recur, and observe how the design and proportions of decorative elements such as mouldings alter to express the character of a period.

I have always found the work of Sir John Soane (1753–1837) fascinating and inspiring. More than any other architect he thoroughly understood how to manipulate volume to create mystery and surprise in an interior. Modern examples can be equally stimulating. I recall my excitement the first time I saw the Seagram Building in New York; I also enjoy the sculptural qualities of the Guggenheim Museum and the Sydney Opera House.

A working familiarity can also be gained by drawing. Reproducing shapes accurately, working to scale, devising different arrangements in plan or elevation will teach you much about proportion, discipline your ideas and introduce you to the idea of thinking architecturally.

CHAPTER THREE

ORGANIZING SPACE

Spaciousness is a great luxury today. This quality, however, is not dependent on size but on proper organization. Practical common sense always dictates good spatial design, enabling the maximum use to be made of the available area. Dead space is a waste of money, for the private individual as much as the public corporation.

Spatial design concerns two main elements: the physical structure and layout of a building, and its architectural detail. Although the former is the preserve of architects and surveyors, especially in the case of structural alterations, designers should work with the architects whenever possible, offering their own insights and suggestions for improvement.

Remodelling or structural alteration has become such a modern preoccupation that it is easy to lose sight of the fact that there is tremendous historical precedent for such an approach. Many great houses have seen centuries of change; few remain exactly as they were first conceived.

There are people today who deplore any significant alteration made to a building, particularly if it is of historic or architectural interest. Indeed, many examples could be cited where both interiors and exteriors have been ruined by heavy-handed, misguided 'improvement'. Buildings, however, generally outlive their original occupants and outlast the functions for which they were built. At least some adaptation, sensitively designed and executed, will always be necessary. What is important is that due care is taken so that changes develop and increase the potential of a space, not obliterate its original qualities.

ARCHITECTURAL DETAIL

Architectural detail is what might be termed the 'immovable furniture' of a room – mouldings, cornices, skirting boards, architraves, chair and picture rails. Today we are in the position to assess the contribution these details make to an interior. After the Second World War, through simple negligence or an ill-advised enthusiasm for modernity, many older houses were stripped of such original features. The results were disastrous. It is clear from these denuded, characterless rooms that detailing serves not only to add decorative interest but to delineate proportion. An important lesson was learned, admittedly the hard way, and there is now much emphasis on restoring architectural detail to interiors and incorporating it in new buildings.

Types of detailing

Each 'detail' has its own aesthetic contribution to make. Many serve a practical function as well.

Skirting boards provide some protection to the base of the plaster-work but, more importantly, give a neat, finished look to a room. Without them, any interior looks incomplete. To preserve the unclut-

Below In this suite in the St Regis Hotel in New York, I did not wish to interfere with the splendid turn-of-the-century plasterwork so, when faced with the need to install shelves, I designed movable, adjustable shelves in chrome, which could simply be wedged between the floor and the ceiling.

tered lines of a modern room, skirting boards can be recessed flush with the wall, with a groove incised along the top edge to give the impression of beading.

In earlier centuries, furniture was often pushed back against the walls, not grouped in informal arrangements as it is today. The chair rail, therefore, was originally a device to prevent the backs of chairs scraping or denting expensive wallpaper or fine fabrics, such as damask, stretched over the walls. The chair rail is usually set about thirty inches from the ground, and has become a classic element in rooms that are tall enough to take it. It provides the opportunity to stop a colour two-thirds of the way down the wall and treat the remainder of the space, including the dado and skirting board, in a different manner.

The picture rail was a Victorian addition. As the name suggests, its purpose was to act as a suspension point for pictures, a function entirely redundant today. I personally do not like picture rails and feel that they make an unfortunate three-quarter break in the wall. If the chair rail is missing, I often move the picture rail down and use it as the chair rail.

Plasterwork mouldings or cornices add interest and character, as well as making a gentle join between the vertical surface of the wall and the horizontal of the ceiling. Architraves, the wooden mouldings around doors and windows, serve much the same function, literally framing an entrance or opening.

The design of such detailing varies according to the period and the grandeur of its setting. In general, Georgian detailing was classically plain and elegant, whereas Victorian examples became increasingly elaborate and ornate. Contemporary pattern books can be consulted to discover typical designs and their variations.

Restoring detailing

Before you consider the type of detailing to put in a room, it is essential to have some idea of the furniture layout and the mood you are setting out to create. Try to respect any existing details which are of good quality and proportion, but do not feel you have to stay rigorously in period. If you are designing a modern interior, the simplicity of neo-classical mouldings would be a sympathetic addition.

If details are missing altogether, there are a number of sources you can visit. The recent revival of interest in restoration and conservation has led to the emergence of architectural salvage companies, which retrieve detailing from demolished buildings. Country-house sales are similar sources; many antique shops carry more portable items, such as ironmongery. Precise matching may be possible by scavenging from local building sites – many older houses were built in developments to a basic pattern and it is likely that houses in your area will have similar detailing.

Damaged plasterwork mouldings can be repaired by asking a plasterer to recast the missing fragments. Some firms carry moulds of common designs; whole sections may be available ready-made. Another typical problem is that the more delicate and ornate a moulding, the more likely it is to have become clogged and obscured with layers of paint over the years. Removing this is a most laborious and time-consuming business. The usual method is to apply water or chemical solvent, depending on the type of paint, and then scrape away gently in the cracks and crevices, using fine tools and small brushes.

STRUCTURAL ALTERATION

Changes to the physical structure and layout of a building fall into two categories: those that can be accomplished without an architect's assistance and those that cannot. Because of the complexities of construction, it is not always easy to tell the two apart.

In a typical house, composed of foundations, floors, walls and roof, each component participates to a different degree in holding the whole structure together. Some elements, such as partition walls, play only a minor role; others, such as external and load-bearing walls, are crucially important to the building's stability. Removing a partition wall, for example, may involve no more than simple building work, but an equivalent change to a load-bearing wall requires the provision of an alternative reinforcement, such as a beam, to compensate for the loss of area. Other changes impose their own demands and, because of the wide-ranging effects such alterations can have, it is always essential to consult an architect or surveyor before planning any physical change to the fabric of the building.

Below An elevation showing handsome panelling detail.

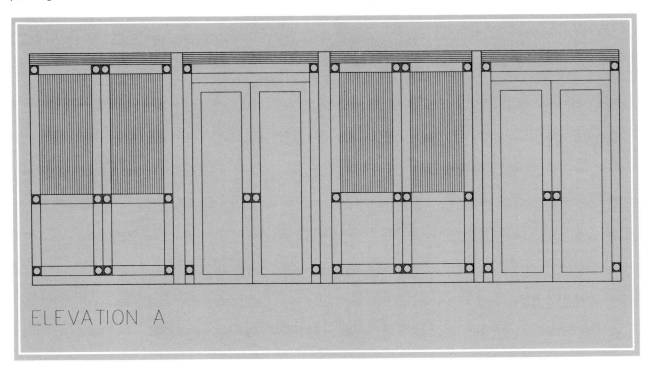

ELEVATION A

Working with architects

In Britain, at least, many structural alterations are subject to building-regulations approval. This means that calculations, usually prepared by a structural engineer, must be submitted to show that sufficient reinforcement will be provided to accommodate the proposed changes.

Other permissions may also be required before work can proceed. These include approval by the landlord or freeholder if the property is an apartment, and planning permission from the local authority, especially if the alteration will affect the external appearance of the building. Changes may also need to comply with health and safety regulations, or fire regulations. Laws applying to historic buildings are particularly stringent. Any house which is 'listed' as being of special historic or architectural merit can often only be changed internally, or sometimes not at all.

Negotiating these technical and bureaucratic labyrinths is much easier with the help of an architect. They are skilled at dealing with consultants such as surveyors and structural engineers, fully informed about current building practices and experienced at handling planning departments. All of this expertise can make the preliminary stages of a job go much more smoothly. If you engage an architect to oversee the work until its completion, they can also help you select a builder, specify the correct materials and check the job as it progresses.

The main role of the architect, however, is to produce a design that meets your requirements. In this capacity the architect works with a client in exactly the same way as the interior designer: establishing a brief, devising a scheme and preparing cost and time estimates.

In any scheme where the client wishes to use both an architect and interior designer, it is absolutely essential that the interior designer is involved right from the beginning. Two minds thinking about spatial design are better than one and the final result is likely to be much more homogeneous and harmonious.

Redesigning layout and circulation

The 'circulation' or flow of traffic about a building affects how the various spaces work. If the traffic flow is confused or awkwardly arranged, you may have both dead, unusable corners and cramped areas where the pressure on space is intense. You will certainly experience daily inconvenience: the house won't feel right or work properly, even if there is theoretically adequate room.

The best way to assess circulation is to make a simple plan of each floor and on it mark all doors, connecting areas, stairways and access points. Then draw in arrows representing common routes from area to area. With experience, you will be able to see at a glance where improvements can be made. The connections between kitchens and dining rooms and between bedrooms and bathrooms are where many problems lie.

One way to improve circulation is to reconsider how your rooms are used. Houses built in earlier periods reflect a way of life which no longer exists, and they may need reorganization to bring them up-to-date with modern requirements. A room nominally designated as a drawing room may be better used as a kitchen, or vice versa; a small spare bedroom may easily be converted into a second bathroom.

In older homes, hallways are often extremely wasteful of space. They can also be awkward and rambling, particularly if the house has accumulated additions and extensions over the years. The problem can be compounded if there are many different doors opening off the same passageway. Blocking up a door is a simple procedure that can improve the appearance of a hall, provide increased wall area and more usable floor space. In a wide hallway, for example, losing a door may create the opportunity to make a dining area; in a kitchen with two points of access, blocking up one of them may make more space available for a countertop or storage units.

If you cannot afford to lose a door, the answer may be to conceal or 'jib' it to simplify the look of the space. Doors can also be rehung so that they open in the other direction and thus save room where it is needed. Another neat solution is to turn a door into a pair of doors by cutting it in half and adding a rebate along the new edges. This adds interest as well as saving space.

A particular layout problem may demand, on the other hand, that you add a new opening between rooms or reposition an existing one. A serving hatch may improve the workability of the kitchen and dining room; a new doorway may be necessary if you decide to partition a room. Although these changes are relatively minor, if the wall concerned is a structural one a lintel or beam may have to be installed, depending on the size of the new opening.

Take care to design new openings to suit the scale of the rooms, finishing them off so they are consistent with the architectural detail elsewhere. Similarly, if you are blocking up an entrance, extend any cornices, skirting boards or chair rails across the new area of wall.

Layout and circulation are equally important in the design of public areas. Here space is often expensive and its potential must be maximized to promote efficiency. At the beginning you should make a careful study of the working methods of those who will use the area, the space they require for various tasks and the traffic flow between common points and entrances. The character of the modern office owes much to this type of research (sometimes called ergonomics), as does the design of office furniture and equipment.

Many offices demand a high degree of flexibility, making open-plan arrangements more suitable than a series of separate rooms. Senior staff, conference areas and receptions, however, are often best allocated distinct spaces; if this is not possible, movable partitions can be used to provide sound insulation and an element of privacy while preserving

Far right A floor plan for a restaurant in the Far East. In addition to the open dining areas, there are alcoves which can be partitioned off with bi-fold doors for private parties.

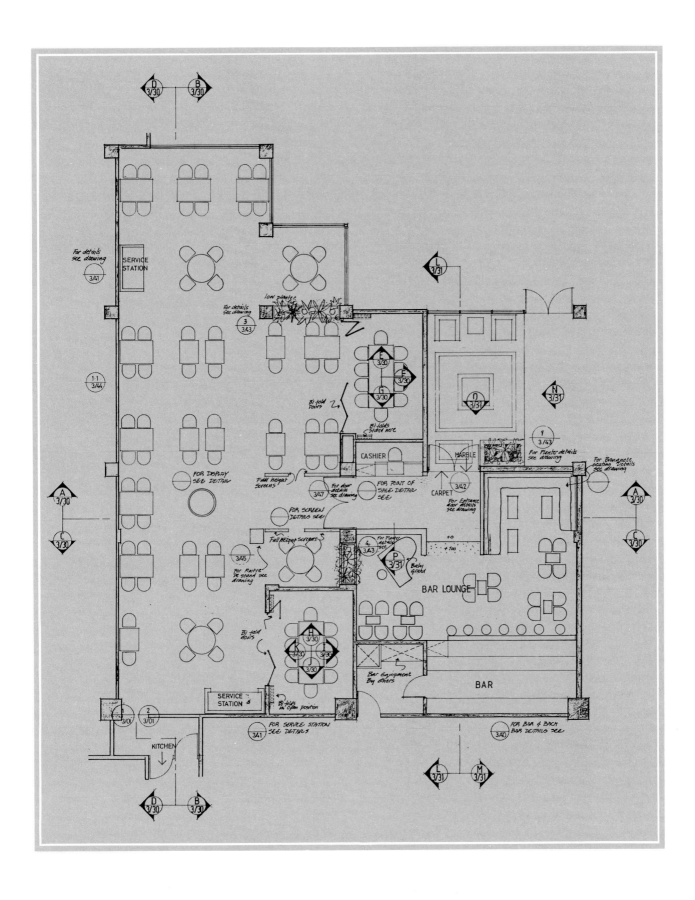

Far left In this bedroom in a Portuguese villa, a jib door holds two architectural prints which are fixed by screws through from the back of the door. Firm fixing is necessary to prevent the pictures from wobbling as the door opens.

Top left An exterior jib door covered with a flush rendered panel of plaster, matching the walls of a loggia.

Below left A jib door concealed by prints.

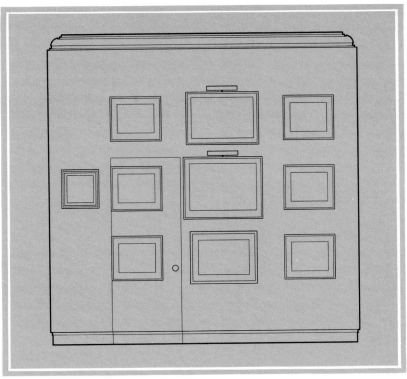

the option of rearranging an area at a later date. Servicing must be carefully planned to allow for such adaptability, which means taking care over electrical and lighting layouts. Trailing wires and over-used sockets are a positive hazard in an office. There are also health and safety regulations to consider, regarding fire-escapes, light levels, ventilation and density (the number of people legally allowed to work in a given area).

Restaurants, hotel foyers and showrooms pose a different type of problem. In many cases, quite distinct activities have to be accommodated within the same area. An important consideration is the interaction of staff and customers. In situations where a desk is required – as in a reception, till or entrance point – its design and position will affect both the control of traffic and general efficiency. Few employees like to work in isolation on an 'island' in the middle of the floor, with the public approaching them from any angle. To enable staff to work effectively and to help control security, desks or work-stations are best placed where there is a wall or partition to act as a screen.

Kitchen layout

The kitchen is the most intensely practical area in the home. Today, it is often necessary to accommodate food preparation, cooking, washing, refuse disposal, storage and even dining all in the same room, whereas in the past, breakfast rooms, sculleries and pantries kept at least some of these activities separate.

Kitchen layout demands rigorous planning. Remember that appliances, work surfaces and storage units today are largely built-in and there will be little opportunity to tinker with an arrangement later. Altering drainage is also complicated and expensive (especially at ground level), which increases the need to get it right from the start.

The main kitchen tasks of preparation (refrigerator, countertop), cooking (hob, oven) and washing (sink) must be related to each other in a workable sequence that allows free movement, yet is not wasteful of space. There are several typical kitchen plans which can be adapted to suit a particular location. In small spaces, a linear arrangement along one wall, or a galley, using two facing walls, is often best. L- or U-shaped plans require more space and are ideally suited to kitchens which incorporate a dining area. For really large kitchens, an island unit in the middle of the room can be very effective. This is a solution commonly adopted by professional cooks.

Kitchen design has become an increasingly specialized field. It has never been one of my main areas of interest and I have designed few during my career. I usually advise clients to consult a good kitchen designer or manufacturer and select a suitable style from one of their ranges. Many manufacturers will plan a layout for you, taking into account the position and dimensions of appliances.

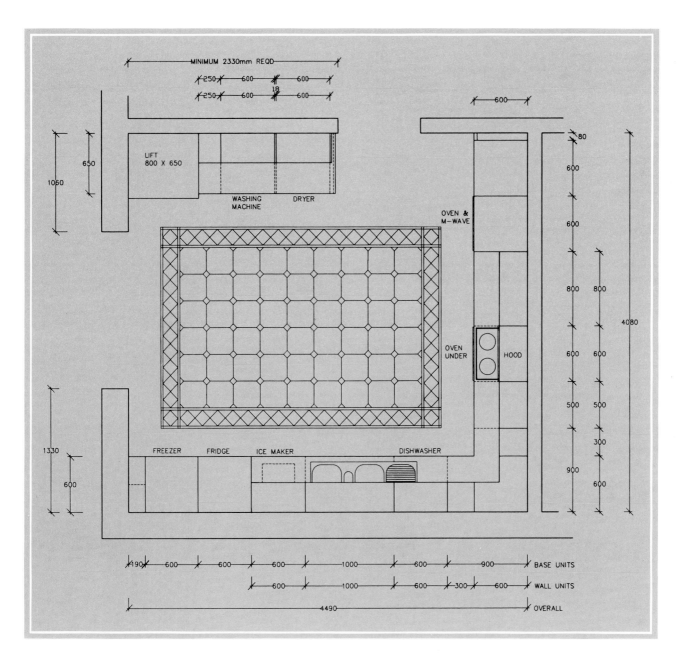

Above This plan for a large and well-equipped kitchen shows the importance of accuracy when integrating units and appliances.

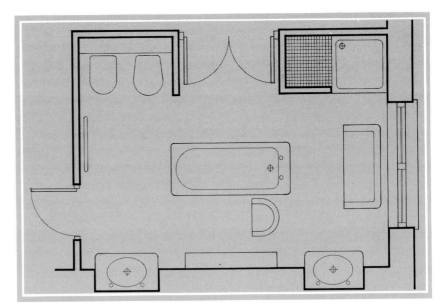

Right Wherever possible – if space and plumbing permit – it is best to interrupt the view from the bathtub to the lavatory. If the room is really large, a bath can be sited in the middle of the space, immediately introducing a note of drama. In more confined areas, the bath and lavatory can be aligned along one wall, partitioned by a screen of some sort, either built-in or something as simple as a towel-rail. Small bathrooms require different solutions. In such cases, the bath can be built into an alcove, which can then be screened by curtaining.

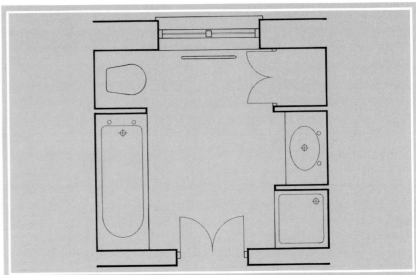

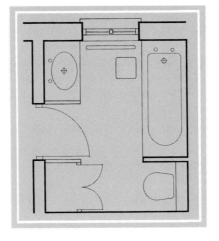

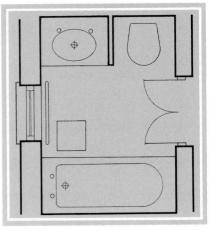

Bathroom layout

Although I don't find kitchens very inspiring, I have devoted much thought to bathroom design. In the beginning this may have been as much to do with self-interest as anything else. Not very long ago bathrooms were neglected places, clinically decorated and awkwardly planned. It was as if the intention was to encourage people to spend little time there and for the experience to be as unpleasant as possible.

All this has changed. I believe I can claim some credit for the recognition in Britain that bathrooms should be furnished, decorated and planned with as much care as the rest of the home. Bathrooms are frequently used and, most importantly, they are where you start and end the day. No one should have to begin and end their daily routine in a room that is uncomfortable, unwelcoming and unattractive.

Above This all-white bathroom in the South of France has a bath inset in an opening, acting as a room divider between the dressing room and bathroom proper. Beyond the bath can be seen a wash-basin with its white cotton skirt and unglazed terracotta vanitory-top. The tomettes (red terracotta tiles) on the floor were painted white.

Bathroom layout is essentially determined by the placing of the lavatory, bath and wash-basin. Although the effects of poor planning are more obvious in the bathroom than anywhere else, builders and plumbers are singularly unimaginative in this respect. And, once the plumbing is completed, alterations can be expensive and disruptive. For these reasons, it is important to be involved in the planning from the beginning.

There is nothing worse than lying in the bath and having to look at the WC. There are several ways of solving this problem. The lavatory, bath and wash-basin, together with the bidet, can be lined up along one wall, with the bath in the centre screened by partitions at either end. The bathtub can also be totally enclosed in an alcove, easily achieved by building out from the wall. If space or budget won't allow such an arrangement, a simple solution is to place a heated towel rail at right angles to the wall between the lavatory and bath, or position the wash-basin between the lavatory and bath to interrupt the view.

Bathrooms of a substantial size can take more imaginative layouts. I have often sited the bathtub in the centre of a room, away from the walls. To achieve the necessary fall for drainage, you simply use the thickness of the floor on which the bath is standing. If the floor does not have enough depth, the bath can be raised on a platform.

Planning storage

Few homes possess enough cupboard or drawer space, and what exists is all too often obtrusive and awkward. Remodelling an interior can provide the perfect opportunity to reassess and improve storage facilities. Adequate, well-organized storage contributes greatly to good spatial design – rooms lose unnecessary, irrelevant clutter and the overall workability of an area increases.

First of all, decide what is to be displayed and what is to be hidden; what must be to hand and what is rarely needed. Remember to allow for occasional demands, such as space for the suitcases of weekend guests, and seasonal variations, such as a winter home for garden furniture. If you have enough space, it may be worth devoting a whole room to storage for items that must be kept but are not in everyday use.

Display is one thing (see page 187), but for objects that must be stored out of sight, I prefer built-in floor-to-ceiling cupboards. You can always place rarely used items on the higher, less accessible shelves. Even in a kitchen there is no point in units that stop at eye-level. Those which don't go right up to the ceiling waste space and inevitably attract dust and clutter.

New cupboards can be sited in redundant alcoves or awkward corners, thus tidying and simplifying the appearance of a room. They should always be treated to blend in with the walls, not made a feature in their own right.

Far right The walls of this bedroom are entirely hung with pleated cotton. Recesses are curtained to conceal hanging space, or, in this instance, shelves for storing shoes. The fabric reefs up on either side like theatre curtains.

Drapery with tails

Overleaf and below A useless flat roof was used to create a dining-room extension to an already large living room, using both clear glass and mirrors for its effect.

Improving spatial quality

The structure of a building dictates not only how it is used, but also the degree of light it receives, the scale and proportion of the spaces within it and its overall atmosphere and character. Physical changes to improve any of these aspects range from simple decorative treatments to major alterations.

'Cosmetic' improvements can involve making the most of a structural obstacle. If there is a boxed-in stack carrying pipes in one corner of a room, simply building another on the opposite side will add symmetry and look considered. If a structural beam cuts across a bedroom ceiling, this could be used to create an alcove for the bed, thus adding to the pleasure and interest of the room. When I designed a nightclub in Glasgow, the site had three iron supporting columns which could not be removed. I added a fourth for symmetry and decorated the room like a marquee, transforming the columns into 'tent poles'.

If a living room needs vertical emphasis, this can be provided by installing floor-to-ceiling cupboards on either side of the chimney breast. If a room is too high, the ceiling can be lowered by building a false one underneath the original.

Mirror is very useful for increasing the sense of space. A large sheet of plain mirror over a chimney piece can look very stylish. It should be as wide as the outer verticals of the chimney breast – not of the mantel-shelf – and extend right up to the underside of the cornice. Similarly, mirror over a bathtub can open up a small bathroom, but it should cover the entire wall, from the tub to the ceiling.

Certain spatial problems call for more radical solutions. Changing walls, windows or levels can dramatically improve an interior but, in most cases, you will need architectural advice. You should also carefully consider the effect such alterations will have on the character of your home. Adding a new window, for example, may brighten up a gloomy room, but if it is not positioned carefully it may ruin the external elevation. And before you knock down walls or partition rooms make sure you are not upsetting the balance between openness and privacy. Most structural work is expensive, disruptive and permanent, so a great deal of careful thought is needed during the planning stage.

Properly considered, however, such changes can be rewarding. I once owned a flat in London which consisted of seven small rooms, none large enough for entertaining. To introduce spaciousness without losing privacy, I demolished two partition walls, creating two large rooms from four, and left the three other rooms as they were. I then linked the two rooms with connecting doors on either side of the chimney breast to produce what the French call *enfilade* – 'looking through'.

Knocking down a wall between two rooms is a common remedy when more space or light is required. A new supporting beam or lintel may need to be installed if the wall is a structural one. I prefer to take the wall right out so that there is no reminder that the room was once divided. An alternative, if you wish to retain the option of closing off the rooms as before, is to make a large, symmetrical opening that can be fitted with double doors. It is cheaper to buy the doors first and then design the opening accordingly.

Partitioning a room demands careful consideration. It is a pity to sacrifice a really splendid room by dividing it up, but the area must nevertheless be large enough so that the two new rooms are habitable and well-proportioned. Plan where the partition will go by making a scale drawing of the existing room, including features such as fire-places, together with windows and doors. The new wall should be positioned so that both rooms have at least one window. L-shaped rooms offer the opportunity to site the partition in the right angle, and some irregularly shaped rooms may actually benefit from being divided. Any architectural details such as cornices or skirting boards should be extended across the new area of wall.

New external openings should be planned with regard to size,

Right A narrow London hall was given more width and storage space by forming a 'Soane-esque' alcove. This contains a fine Regency marble-topped table. There are jib doors to the left and right.

position and style. Since external walls are important structural elements, such an alteration usually requires the addition of a supporting beam or lintel. However, making a new window or installing French doors may be the only way to increase the light, exploit a good view or westerly aspect, or integrate a living area with the garden.

Some designers and many architects are particularly fond of building galleries in rooms high enough to take them, or cutting away a portion of the floor to make a double-height space. I personally find that this only creates problems – the result is difficult to heat and rarely increases usable floor area.

The ultimate structural alteration is, of course, building on to a house – either a new storey, a new room such as a conservatory or even an entire wing. Here the cardinal rule is that whatever is added must be sympathetic in terms of construction, materials and design to the existing building. Access must also be carefully considered to make the new area a true extension of space, not an untidy afterthought. In many areas, planning laws are quite strict about where extensions can be built and how high they can be, especially if they are visible from the street.

Left The transforming potential of mirror glass is shown in the treatment of this typically small New York bathroom on Fifth Avenue. Every conceivable surface was mirrored, creating an illusion of space and depth.

CHAPTER FOUR

LIGHTING

Electric lighting plays a dual role in the interior. First, it is functional, enabling everyday activities to be performed safely in the absence of adequate natural light. Secondly, it is decorative, accenting objets d'art and paintings, creating warmth and atmosphere and revealing contrasts of texture, shape and colour. To meet all these requirements, lighting must be subtle, practical and adaptable.

Natural light is the standard by which artificial light should be judged. Daylight is remarkably varied and visually stimulating compared with man-made versions. The low sun at dawn or dusk has golden, rosy tints; at noon on a clear day the sun casts strong, direct shadows; by contrast, light filtered through cloud cover has a soft, even tone. And light also varies in different parts of the world, a quality which has long been appreciated by artists. To supplement or substitute for natural light, artificial light must re-create some of this richness and variety, not only in tone, but also in direction, level and intensity.

Using lighting successfully demands careful planning. You must take into account the degree and quality of the existing natural light, consider the layout and position of light sources, the type of illumination (intensity, spread and direction) and the design of fitting and shade. Fortunately, advances in technology have ensured that a broad range of domestic lighting is available today, to suit every taste and budget.

CONTROLLING NATURAL LIGHT

The amount of natural light a room receives forms the context in which a lighting scheme should be planned. Existing daylight will be determined by the aspect, climate and size of the windows, but the quality of this light can be adjusted to increase drama and interest. Daylight filtered by curtains, blinds or shutters is much more flattering to people, objects and furniture. These options are also practical, providing privacy, prolonging the life of pictures and printed fabrics, and insulating a room against sound and heat loss or gain.

A wide range of solutions can be adopted; specific curtain and blind treatments will be discussed in the chapter on soft furnishing (see page 132). Most beautiful rooms look better with the windows partially covered and the light coming in from low down. Inspiration can be taken from Mediterranean and Far Eastern interiors, where the heat and glare of the sun is screened in many interesting ways – think of the charm of a patio shaded by *canisse* (split cane), or a balcony shuttered with wooden louvres. A similar type of atmosphere can be created by using exterior blinds, grilles, smoked glass, fine venetian blinds, holland, Roman or festoon blinds. A permanent trellis-type screen can look well in a modern interior. Your choice should depend on the style of the room, but you should always avoid that time-worn solution of net curtains, especially those that are staggered or swagged. If you must have net, use fine white tulle gathered thickly and hung straight. Lace curtains can be charming in a Victorian villa but, like nets, these must be straight and full. A nicer alternative is to hang café curtains of thin white poplin or cotton from a brass pole halfway up the window.

In more functional areas such as bathrooms and kitchens, light should not be filtered to an impractical degree. Flexibility is important. Venetian blinds, which may seem a natural choice, are notoriously difficult to clean and should be avoided. Café curtains are fresh-looking and much easier to maintain, as are holland blinds.

Ideally, all curtains, especially those in bedrooms, should be inter-lined, and then lined in black as well as ordinary lining to screen light out completely. At night the ugly glare of street-lighting can penetrate and ruin the effect you are trying to create.

TYPES OF LIGHTING

Before planning a lighting installation, you should familiarize yourself with the types of lights available and the jobs they are designed to do. A light consists of two basic elements: the light source, or bulb, and the fitting.

Technically, natural light is designated 'white'. Compared with this standard, all other light sources produce a colour cast. None has yet been designed that enables us to see colours as they really are, but the degree of distortion varies widely.

The most popular and enduring light source is the tungsten bulb.

This is available in clear or pearl glass, and gives a warm, yellowish light that makes it particularly sympathetic in the interior. Its disadvantages are that it does generate a fair degree of heat and has a limited life.

A recent development is the tungsten halogen bulb. This is cooler and whiter than tungsten and, although it is not suitable for general use, it is effective in spotlights or uplighters, or wherever crisp, concentrated light is needed.

The third type of light source is the fluorescent bulb or tube. Despite manufacturers' claims that new types are whiter and less insistent, I still find fluorescent light to be totally unsuitable for home or office use. It *is* cheap, bright and long-lasting, but also cold, brash and with a significant green cast that distorts the colour of food and merchandise. In a working environment it is tiring, relentless and aggravating. Many people complain of headaches after working under fluorescent light for only a few hours.

The effect of the light source is determined by the design of the light fitting (sometimes known as the luminaire). At one extreme, lighting can be highly directional, concentrated in a beam to accent a working area, picture or decorative detail. At the other, lighting can be totally diffused so that it provides general background illumination. Most lights fall somewhere between the two; that is, the majority of the light goes in one direction but a quantity diffuses or spills in other directions. This is the typical effect of a table lamp.

Left For Lady Cook, I devised an oeil de boeuf window in the bathroom, glazing it with frosted glass, since the room overlooked a neighbouring property.

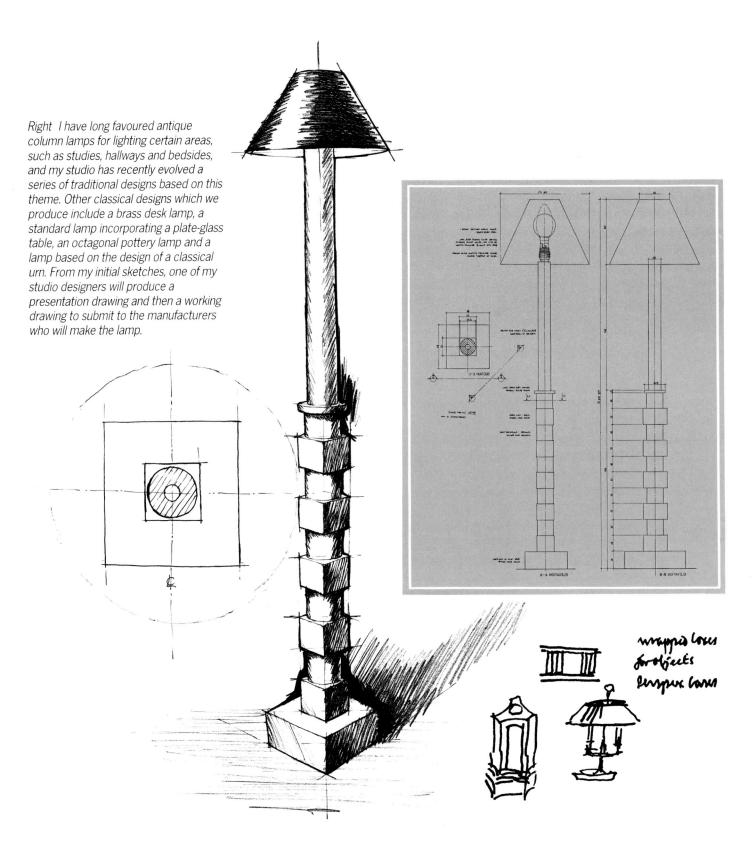

*Right I have long favoured antique
column lamps for lighting certain areas,
such as studies, hallways and bedsides,
and my studio has recently evolved a
series of traditional designs based on this
theme. Other classical designs which we
produce include a brass desk lamp, a
standard lamp incorporating a plate-glass
table, an octagonal pottery lamp and a
lamp based on the design of a classical
urn. From my initial sketches, one of my
studio designers will produce a
presentation drawing and then a working
drawing to submit to the manufacturers
who will make the lamp.*

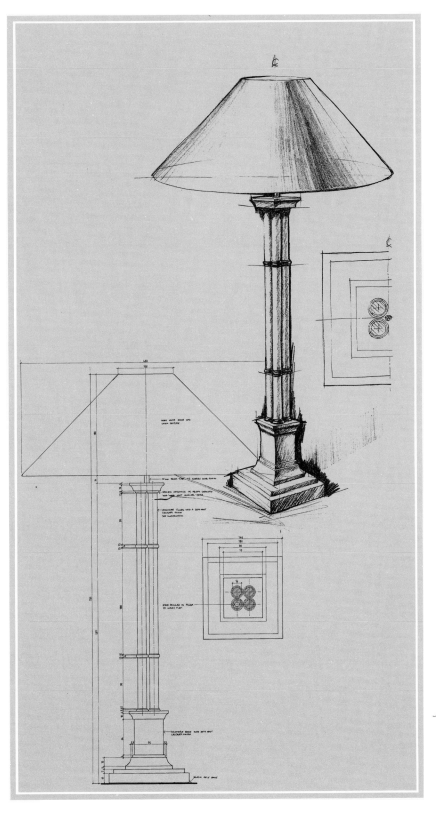

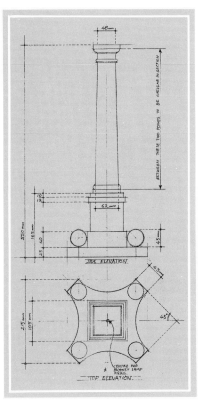

Lighting design has almost become a science, and terminology can be confusing. Rather than becoming mired in technicalities, the best way to assess the qualities of different lights is to visit a good lighting showroom and see for yourself what is on the market. People often make the mistake of choosing a light on the strength of its appearance alone; before you make up your mind always turn it on to see the effect it creates.

As a brief guide, the following are typical categories of lights and their uses:

Downlighters   These are directional lights, usually recessed in the ceiling, which are unobtrusive in design, and excellent for use in kitchens and bathrooms, or for illuminating working areas. They have become a modern classic, invaluable in many situations, and are widely available today.

Uplighters   Uplighters, as the name suggests, direct all their light to the ceiling, adding to the general level of illumination. I first saw uplighters in 1957 when I visited Philip Johnson's Glass House in New Canaan, Connecticut. At that time they were not made in Britain and had to be imported. The simple designs look well in most interiors. They are often fitted with halogen bulbs and can be wall-mounted or stood on the floor.

Wall lights   These are often mounted on the walls in pairs, and give a discreet background light. Some are designed to simulate candle sconces; if so, the false candles must be at least eight to twelve inches long, which they never are, so you will have to alter them.

Ceiling lights   These range from lights mounted on the ceiling to pendants and chandeliers which are suspended from it. Most ceiling lighting is avoidable – overhead light flattens shadows and destroys atmosphere. If the room is grand enough to take it, an electric chandelier can be an exciting focal point. This must have long false candles, with the bulbs always shaded.

Spotlights   There are a wide variety of spotlights available: eyeball, parabolic, wall-washers, which flood an area of wall, spotlights mounted on tracks or upright stands. I often direct parabolic spotlights to highlight sculptures or other objects; their silvered bulbs partially disguise the light source.

Striplighting   Useful for concealed lighting – beneath kitchen units or even above a deep cornice – striplights consist of a tube, often fluorescent. However, tungsten strips are also available, which are much more suitable in the home. The light source must always be hidden behind a baffle or in a recess.

Far right This sitting room in Athens has the benefit of strong natural light by day. At night, the lighting is equally dramatic. Four clusters of parabolic spotlights look attractive as well as being highly practical, and do not detract from the amusing amber and crystal chandelier.

Picture lights   I like old-fashioned picture lights coming out on arms from the back of the picture frame. They produce a warm, cosy atmosphere and enhance the painting. Mini-projectors, mounted in the ceiling, can be masked exactly to the canvas size, but they produce a rainbow effect around the edge and make good pictures look like reproductions.

Standard lights   These upright lights, which stand on the floor and are rather like over-sized table lamps, can have a stuffy, dated look. Plain designs are best if you need one to read by or to light a bridge table.

Desk lights   A variety of good designs are produced, from the classic column lamp to curved brass Victorian lamps with green glass shades.

Table lamps   Table lamps are the mainstay of domestic lighting schemes. Always use pearl bulbs, to prevent a shadow repeat on the ceiling of the shade carrier. I often place unpainted copper discs on the shade carrier to direct light down onto the table and keep the light off the ceiling.

DEVISING A LIGHTING LAYOUT

Lighting should be planned with reference to the furniture arrangement, and related to areas of use, such as work surfaces, seating, bedsides and wash-basins. Until you know what the furniture layout is going to be, it is impossible to make firm decisions about the position of lights, points and switches.

As always, scale drawings are invaluable. A good plan will help you site points conveniently and thus avoid trailing flexes. Nowadays, one is not allowed to install a socket in the skirting board – although this looks neater, it is not considered safe. An electrician will be able to advise on the recommended height for points above the floor or work surface. More important than their actual position, however, is making sure you have enough of them. The reasons are not only aesthetic: an overloaded socket is a hazard.

Consult the furniture plan to make sure all important areas are served with light. A neat solution may suggest itself. For example, a sideboard may be the perfect place for a table lamp, with the point concealed behind and the wire taped down the back of one leg. Or a point with a sprung-metal cover could be installed in the floor next to a seating arrangement.

Similarly, elevations are useful for judging the position of spotlights, wall-mounted fittings, picture lights and switches. I like to control all lights and points from one switch near the door, fitted with a dimmer to adjust the light level. Such a wiring arrangement is only marginally more expensive if it can be built in during conversion work; otherwise, it can be disruptive and costly. Switches look best about three feet above the floor, aligned with the chair rail if there is one.

Remember that quite strict regulations apply in the case of bathrooms. The main light switch must be outside the door. If the room is large enough to take a table lamp, it must be wired straight into the socket, not fitted with a conventional plug. These restrictions are designed to keep water well away from electricity.

In children's rooms, place switches higher up the wall, well out of reach. Protect points with socket covers when they are not in use.

LIGHTING WITH STYLE

When I was thirteen I cut a laminate (there was little plastic in 1942) washing-up bowl in half and made two wall lights. How I got them fixed to the wall I cannot remember, but they provided a luxurious source of indirect light for my studio (which was, in fact, a pre-war treble garage that I had converted). I still cannot bear to see the source of light.

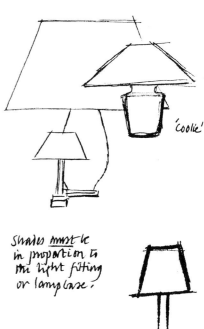

'coolie'

As well as being indirect, lighting must also be varied. Any surface that is smoothly lit looks boring; it is the interplay of light and shade that generates interest. Many different sources of light create overlapping, concentrated pools of light, a subtlety entirely missing if a room is evenly illuminated by a single bright overhead fixture. In the same way, using light to pick out objects or an architectural detail such as a cornice is highly dramatic and theatrical, emulating the effect of a strong shaft of early or late sunlight. The only exceptions are in work areas such as kitchens or offices, where the emphasis is on safety and efficiency, not atmosphere. Even in such a location, however, it is possible to design an installation that is sympathetic rather than harshly functional.

Shades must be in proportion to the light fitting or lamp base.

Non-electric light sources also have their own particular charm. Firelight instantly creates an intimate mood; candlelight is subtle and complimentary. I insist on shading candles, just as I always shade bare bulbs. The best design consists of a conical metal shade in spun aluminium mounted on a brass fitting that imperceptibly slips down the candle as it burns, and prevents it from guttering. For parties, you can mass candles of different heights and thicknesses – but always use proper white or tallow-coloured ones – the coloured varieties look vulgar. And never buy barley-twist, tapered or gold-flecked types.

Living rooms

Most average-sized living rooms need at least four table lamps. Although many people try to do with less, this only means that each source has to be stronger to provide adequate illumination. It is better to have more lights, each of a lower wattage, rather than a few really bright, glaring ones. On the other hand, too many lamps can make a room look cluttered.

Table lamps are such an important component of domestic lighting that it is worth discussing their design in detail. The simple, classic shapes are the best, colour-coordinated with the decorative scheme. Many bases are much too fussy and ornate, especially some contemporary designs. A degree of elaboration looks right if the lamp is antique but it is hard to go wrong with simple white pottery or other plain-coloured ones.

The proportion of base to shade must also be finely judged. Too small or too large a shade makes the whole lamp look absurd. In general, lamps should be between fourteen and twenty-four inches in height.

I prefer extremely plain, opaque white card shades. Pleated cotton or silk also looks well, and can be interlined with black so the shade is not translucent. Colours should be limited to the neutral tones of white, off-white, beige, dark brown or black, but a small patterned chintz, or pleated batik can be very atmospheric. To add warmth to the light, the shade can be lined in pink.

Attractive table lamps can be made by converting a vase or pair of Edwardian or Victorian candlesticks. In the case of a vase, the bulb holder is fitted into the neck by means of a stopper. To convert candlesticks, insert a piece of copper tube painted white to simulate the candle, and fix the bulb holder to that. The flex is threaded down the tube and out at the side.

Dramatic living-room lighting can be achieved by a judicious placing of uplighters and downlighters. Place uplighters behind pieces of furniture or large plants; downlighters should be recessed wherever possible. Many excellent, plain designs are available; avoid the gimmicks. Spotlights can be used to pinpoint areas of interest, such as a flower or table arrangement. Although these types of light are essentially directional, they increase the general level of illumination and obviate the need for wall lights or ceiling fixtures.

Avoid imitation wall brackets with dripping simulated candles and parchment shades. Opt instead for the classically simple wall fitting in metal, glass or ceramic, but remember that any wall light restricts the area where you can hang pictures.

Unwanted wall-light points can be useful for picture lights, another subtle form of illumination. The light itself should be scaled to fit the painting, not the frame. Parabolic spotlights in the ceiling make good picture lights if you do not want to install points in the wall.

Dining rooms
The object of lighting in a dining room is to produce an intimate atmosphere with no glare. This is one of the few situations where hanging lights can be effective, especially a good chandelier. Chandeliers look best with real candles: if they are electrified, the bulbs must be tiny and shaded. An alternative is to place a group of eyeball spotlights in the ceiling above the table, directed onto a single candle, flower arrangement or centrepiece. Lamps will also be necessary to light the sideboard or serving area.

Left and below Day and night views of my old suite at the St Regis Hotel, New York. The lighting was achieved by using two uplighters, a pair of table lamps on either side of the sofa and a desk light.

Far right A glittering entrance hall in London combines the clever use of lighting with many reflective surfaces. Parabolic spotlights in the ceiling and a pair of candlestick lamps are reflected in the mirror. A collection of Persian silver standing on an Italian silvered console table with a lapis lazuli top sparkles in the light.

Bedrooms

Table lamps and adjustable wall-mounted lights are often the best solution here, particularly on either side of the bed, for reading. Dressing tables and chests of drawers should also be well lit; spotlights and downlighters can be very effective and unobtrusive. Dimmer switches are essential.

Children's rooms

Downlighters are excellent for children's rooms – adjustable, safe and practical. Avoid delicate lamps that can be knocked over. Sturdy angled desk lights are practical for the older child, to light a hobby area or worktop.

Kitchens

The three main areas – stove, sink and countertop – need bright, even light which is safe to work by. Spotlights mounted on ceiling tracks can be directed where light is required; downlighters are also practical. Tungsten strip lights can be mounted beneath eye-level units above the work surface; if you cannot make a recess for these, mask the glare with a wooden or metal baffle. Additional, softer lighting may be required for adjacent dining areas.

Bathrooms

Hanging fittings are unsuitable in bathrooms, since they may be accidentally splashed with water. Central ceiling fixtures, although commonplace, often produce a harsh, unfortunate light which is neither flattering nor relaxing. For general illumination, downlighters are again a good solution; in large bathrooms, table lamps can be used, provided they are wired straight into the socket.

To light a mirror, it is hard to improve on the 'star's dressing room' arrangement, where two rows of opaque bulbs flanks the glass, providing a clear and efficient spread of light for shaving or applying makeup. A single strip light at the top of the mirror is not as effective, since it casts the lower part of the face into shadow.

Entrances, passageways and stairs

Overhead lighting – hanging lights or ceiling fixtures – can be effective and practical in the connecting areas of the home. For safety reasons, lighting here must be even and reasonably bright – too subtle or directional an illumination could be hazardous.

Outdoor lighting

Good exterior lighting serves several functions. It enables you to negotiate the path or drive safely, gives a welcoming, attractive look and can even be highly dramatic if the plants in the surrounding area are worthy of attention.

Far left The best illumination for a bathroom mirror is that originated in stars' dressing rooms, where bulbs are set around the perimeter and light the face from every angle.

Left Glass shelves in front of mirrored alcoves are lit with downlighters recessed into the ceiling in this small London house. A wide sheet of mirror over the early-nineteenth-century chimneypiece adds to the atmospheric effect.

Below This pine-panelled card room in a New York apartment needed an injection of life, so I painted the interiors of the bookshelves with white lacquer and persuaded the client to place objects and drawings among the books. The use of many individual sources of light makes the display interesting and dramatic.

Many mistakes are made in this area, reproduction carriage lamps and coloured lights being among the most common. Light fittings should be discreet – a bulb set into a box and covered with a metal louvre will direct light down on to the steps or path without being obtrusive. Avoid orange light at all costs – it will spoil the appearance of your house as surely as it ruins that of public buildings.

A wide range of garden lighting is now available, ranging from waterproof silvered spotlights which can be directed at the underside of trees, to portable spiked lights that can add a touch of theatre to a festive occasion. Safety is an important consideration: lights must be weather-proof and kept free of debris.

Public contracts
Many public commissions call for imaginative lighting. My design for Le Carosse, a London restaurant, featured small glass showcases mounted on the walls, containing pieces of harness, each lit by a small picture light. In general, each table must also be individually lit, which means the lighting layout must be flexible enough to accommodate alterations to the floor plan. Spotlights, fitted with silvered bulbs to cut glare, can be every effective.

Spotlights, together with downlighters, are also suited to most offices. In fact, track lights were first developed for commercial use, and were subsequently adapted to domestic interiors. In addition to a good general level of background illumination, each desk or work area should have its own light. Angled desk lamps are a modern classic, and hard to better.

Far left Long narrow spaces such as this hallway are always a problem. Here I used a geometric carpet to give character and interest. Parabolic spotlights create drama and dissolve angles. The group of four intaglios on the end wall draws the eye towards it.

CHAPTER FIVE

SURFACE TREATMENTS

Decorating the basic structure of a house or apartment is all too often seen as a necessary but uninteresting preliminary before the pleasurable, creative work of arranging furniture, hanging pictures and grouping objects can begin. But the treatment of the principal surfaces – floors, walls and ceilings – forms more than just a background or context; it actually defines how the entire scheme will develop.

One reason for this is the sheer extent of the area involved. Whatever colour or material you choose for a floor covering, for example, is bound to have a dominant effect simply because there is so much of it.

There is a practical side as well. Different materials or finishes suit different locations, increasing the workability of a room, minimizing maintenance and adding to the overall level of comfort and enjoyment.

The range of solutions, potential materials and treatments is vast. In recent years there has been a remarkable expansion in the quality and design of the products available for almost every surface, from carpeting and synthetic floor tiles to paint and patterned paper. A common reaction to this is to take the easy route: lay a wall-to-wall neutral carpet and paint everything white. This may be uncontroversial, but it is also dull. A bit of serious research into what is currently available will throw up many more exciting alternatives.

One aspect of surface decoration is uninspiring and unavoidable, and that is good preparation. If you prepare surfaces well, your work will be invisible; if you don't, your neglect will be all too obvious. No decoration, however immaculate, can compensate for chipped woodwork or uneven plaster; in fact, it will only highlight superficial irregularities. Bear in mind when deciding what colour to paint your living room that the success of your choice will eventually depend on a sound foundation – and enough time and money should be devoted to this 'hidden' dimension.

FLOORS

In many ways floors are the most important surface in the home, and there is a good argument for making the choice of floor covering your first decision. The floor has an enormous impact on any scheme, both aesthetically and practically, and is also likely to be the single most expensive element. It is infinitely better to plan your decoration around a particular floor than find your options severely restricted in terms of colour, design and material.

Above all, flooring must meet the practical demands of a particular location. Many of the materials best suited to an entrance hall, for example, would be inappropriate in a bedroom.

Whatever solutions you adopt, try to build in interesting contrasts of texture. Since it is often better to keep to natural or muted shades to allow a floor to work with successive schemes – remember that it will outlive the paintwork – textural variety will provide the necessary stimulation.

Despite the technological advances of recent years, nothing will ever match the wonderful floors of the past. The painted wooden floor-boards in American colonial houses, intricate inlaid Georgian parquet, the polished plaster floors of Directoire villas and eighteenth-century palaces and the elaborate geometry of porphyry, lapis and verd-antique in San Marco, Venice, have been a constant inspiration to me. Simplified, updated versions of these classic conceptions can still display something of the same delight in material and pattern.

It is best to choose a floor covering in the context of the overall scheme, not just a particular room. The key point to watch is the

Far left Banding can give a room definition and style. In this foyer, the reception desk has banded panels, and the floor has an inset border which follows the contours of the border on the ceiling, accentuating the architectural details and giving distinction.

Left Details of a table leg and flooring in a Piccadilly showroom.

junction between different types of floor – try not to run two patterned carpets together unless they are harmonious in design or linked by common colours. And remember that the same flooring throughout will unify and increase the sense of space; a variety of treatments will define and enclose areas.

Entrances

The entrance takes the brunt of household activity, with people constantly arriving and departing. Consequently, the floor here must wear well, and show as little dirt from the street or mud from the garden as possible. It should also be relatively easy to maintain.

Since the entrance or hall is the first thing visitors see, it should give a hint of what is to come in terms of style, without making abrupt contrasts with the rooms leading off it. The ideal treatment is often a geometric design, using a combination of materials. This type of floor gives a crisp, cool effect and is practical as well as attractive.

In the city or the country, a generous door-mat is essential. Rubber-backed door-matting is available in different widths, so you can run it wall to wall; it should be as long as the width of the entrance itself. If your budget will allow, inset the mat so that it is flush with the remainder of the floor.

For the rest of the floor, there is a wide variety of materials from which to choose: scrubbed stone, glazed terracotta, slate, marble, brick, vinyl tiles, carpet and scrubbed oak, along with many others. If the area is big enough, define it with an inset or flanking border.

A splendid floor can be the sole decorative feature of an entrance. Some of the best entrance floors I have devised have relied on combining materials in an unexpected way. In a château in Switzerland I designed a bold geometric hall floor in travertine, slate and scrubbed white marble. In 1961 I did a white vinyl-tiled entrance floor inlaid with polished brass borders, with a cipher in the centre also framed by a circular border of brass banding. I am currently working on a villa in the Algarve where the large entrance hall has a classical design of hammered stone octagons, intersections in glazed red terracotta tiles and scrubbed oak banding.

Stairs

Stairs are inevitably best carpeted, both to keep down the noise and to give a sense of comfort. The width of the carpet is open to question – it can either be inset or not, depending on the width of the treads. Stair rods are handsome, but since they are also expensive and need maintenance, it may be more practical to do without them. Avoid coir (coconut matting) or rush matting on the stairs – being slippery underfoot.

Far left Here a long narrow hall needed to be broken up visually. I formed a shallow recess which was mirrored. The surrounds of the alcoves were painted white but a strong colour used for the intervening areas of wall. The whole area is united by a bold geometric carpet and flanking border.

Living rooms

In northern climates, the most popular treatment for living-room floors is undoubtedly carpet. It is warm, luxurious and available in a host of colours, textures and patterns. The best carpets are all wool, but a mix which includes a percentage of artificial fibres is equally acceptable, since this promotes easy maintenance and longevity. All carpets – either wall-to-wall or area rugs – must have good underlay; I prefer felt. Underlay extends the life of a carpet and evens out imperfections in the floorboards so the carpet lies flat and cuts down noise.

When I began my career there were no patterned carpets on the market that were at all sympathetic. Those that were available looked as though a naughty child had thrown several pots of different coloured paint onto a coffee-coloured background, and not as successfully as Jackson Pollock. In the early 1960s I discovered a factory in Yorkshire that had the capacity to produce Brussels weave, a type of wool carpet with a tight uncut loop pile. The factory had already been used successfully by John Fowler to manufacture copies of fragments that he had found in historic houses.

My first two designs were produced in 1961; both were geometrics, based on a 'Y' motif found in a mosque in Persia and in the geometric pattern on the floor of San Marco in Venice. One of these was a simple vermilion line on beige; the other, more complicated one, was black, brown and beige and had greater depth. In the same year I commissioned two textured rugs, one made in Hong Kong in emerald green and white, the other all stone colour, with the pattern achieved by high-cut relief, low relief and uncut ground was made at Cogolins. I used all four in my country house.

Clients soon approached me to ask if I would design carpets for them and, within a short time, I was initiating new designs, most of which were woven in Brussels weave. Later, especially for restaurants and offices, I had designs woven in Wilton quality – cut pile.

After I had produced about a dozen designs, an American wholesaler visited the Yorkshire factory and asked me to produce a complete collection for the American designer market. The collection duly appeared and was a tremendous success, so much so that it is still being sold today. All the carpets are custom-woven, and designers can specify their own colour-ways.

Modern houses and apartments usually look best with the carpeting extended wall-to-wall. If there is a hearth, it should be flush with the carpet, not raised above it. Bind or trim the edge with a lacquered brass strip.

To introduce variety and lend definition, the carpet can include a flanking border. This can provide not only interesting contrasts of colour and pattern but also of texture when a different type of weave is used. A plain Wilton border with a field (or main part) of Brussels weave can look well, as can plain Wilton with a patterned border.

Left Dark colours can dissolve the angles of a room. Here dark walls make a dramatic background for a white marble fireplace and the geometric textured carpet is set off by a wide, dark border.

Below The drawing room at Britwell Salome was quite large in scale. To evoke a cosy, lived-in atmosphere, I covered the floor in a textured carpet and devised a muted colour scheme. The fine chimney surround dates from 1750.

I also use plain natural materials such as jute, rush matting and drugget. In a country house in Ireland, for example, I covered the floor of a huge, long gallery in jute matting, an unusual, inexpensive treatment that was an interesting foil for the fine eighteenth-century furniture and grand architectural features.

In old houses, if the original floor is attractive and sound, it may be better to have area or antique rugs rather than completely covering the floor. Unfortunately, the most acceptable antique rugs are also the earliest and rarest. Persian rugs produced after 1790 generally display ugly colour combinations: gloomy, inky blues, wine reds and faded golds. However, English turkey carpets fom the mid-nineteenth century are generally rich and glowing, and more affordable than the best Persians.

The most economical, practical and popular area rugs are dhurries: Indian carpets woven in cotton or silk. These are available in fresh colours and charming geometric designs; they are also easy to clean. Their only disadvantage is that they are so popular today that they have lost a degree of their originality and impact. I first began to use dhurries in the early 1960s, after a visit to India. While I was there, the Maharani of Jaipur had shown me a selection of traditional dhurries, which were then produced in mundane patterns and muddy colours. On my return home I sent out colour-ways and designs and subsequently marketed the new dhurries through my showrooms.

Aside from dhurries, there are a number of interesting textured rugs from Greece and North Africa, available in plain, natural shades. Choose one large rug rather than several smaller ones, which will make the room look untidy. Underlay will prevent the rug from slipping and also prolong its life.

A good wooden floor can also be attractive in a living room. I prefer strip or plank floors, rather than parquet or wood tiles. Wooden floors should not be varnished to that ubiquitous tea colour: they can be bleached to a pale tone, ebonized to a rich black sheen, stained or painted.

Dining rooms

The main point about the dining-room floor is that it must be easy to maintain. Spills and accidents are inevitable, so any surface which marks or damages easily is not suitable. Neither are hard materials such as stone or ceramic, since whatever you drop on such a surface will inevitably break.

A polished wooden floor with a large antique or modern rug is a good solution here, but remember that a really fine rug will be under constant threat. A patterned wall-to-wall carpet is an alternative treatment; the pattern will also help to disguise marks.

Bedrooms

For warmth and comfort underfoot, wall-to-wall carpeting is a good choice in the bedroom. Or, if there is an attractive, original wooden floor, this can be painted or stained to suit the decoration. A simple stencilled border can add charm.

Children's rooms need tougher flooring – wall-to-wall cord carpet is ideal and makes a safe, practical surface for playing. Choose darkish, neutral colours to hide marks. You can add colour with an inexpensive area rug, but this must be secured to prevent accidents.

Kitchens

Kitchen flooring has come a long way in design and practicality in recent years. As in the dining room, the floor must not be too hard – stone, brick, ceramic or quarry tiles are tiring to stand on for long periods and, again, whatever you drop will break.

Today there are excellent designs available in artificial materials such as vinyl and linoleum, in either tile or sheet form. Many of these simulate natural materials, the best of which include versions of travertine, and the stone octagon and slate dot pattern. Cork tiles are also warm, easy to maintain and attractive.

Wooden floors are also acceptable. The ideal would be unvarnished elm planks, scrubbed with soap and water to achieve a pale, beige colour. Pine floors, sealed or bleached, are attractive, clean and warm.

In a small city apartment, especially if the kitchen is not subject to heavy use, a cord carpet in a dark colour can be surprisingly practical.

Bathrooms

To promote a luxurious, furnished atmosphere in the bathroom, I prefer to carpet it wall-to-wall, either in cord or Brussels weave. Contrary to popular belief, carpet is not impractical in the bathroom; with a large, absorbent bathmat, it shouldn't get too wet and it will not rot. In warmer climates, I sometimes use hard materials such as terrazzo, scrubbed or polished marble or wood, adding a textured plain rug for comfort. In a family bathroom, vinyl or cork tiles are practical, non-slip and water-resistant.

If the bathroom is large enough, an inset border of contrasting colours or materials can give style. A band of unfilled travertine, for example, can be very exciting inset into a polished beige marble floor.

Public contracts

The extent of the surface area generally calls for economic flooring. Carpet, since it insulates against noise and draughts, is easy to maintain and long-lived, is a practical choice. Many carpets are available in heavy-duty weights, which resist wear through constant traffic.

Plain, neutral shades are a common solution, but if the budget or scale of the project allows, it is more interesting to design an original pattern. This can be based on a corporate motif, in a boardroom, perhaps, or pursue a decorative theme in a restaurant or foyer.

WALLS AND CEILINGS

Paint, paper, fabric, panelling, tiles – the scope of finishes available for the other principal surfaces in the interior can seem daunting. To narrow the field, spend enough time at the planning stage to identify the effect you are trying to create. Study the proportions and details of the rooms in question and decide which elements to accentuate and which to disguise. Once you have a clear idea of the atmosphere that is required as well as a sound appreciation of the practicalities involved, you can then consider which materials, colours and patterns would best solve the problem.

As mentioned previously, a scheme board is an invaluable aid to working out a decorative treatment (see page 00). Don't plan a room in isolation, even if it is the only room you intend to change. There should be a sense of flow and connection from area to area.

Paint

Paint is clean, cheap and easy to apply – deservedly the most popular interior finish. Mistakes are simple to rectify, too – a wall can be quickly repainted if the colour looks wrong. Current manufacturers' ranges provide a wealth of shades from which to choose, eliminating the need for special mixing and tinting. Paint is also available in a variety of textures – matt, eggshell and gloss – which introduces even more scope to the effects you can create.

There is a rough set of rules for using paint in the interior. Generally, walls are best painted with an eggshell, or matt, finish, with mid-sheen used on the woodwork. If the walls are in good condition, gloss can be highly effective and lacquer-like, in which case, use matt-texture paint for the detail. I sometimes trim shiny walls with a broad matt jute braid or use two lines of petersham ribbon for a triple band effect, painting between with a third colour.

Ceilings are almost always best painted white or off-white. I usually do the cornices, architraves, skirtings, picture rails and dados, if they exist, white too. In certain circumstances, this rule can be reversed: for example, white walls with pale, stone-coloured trim. Elaborate plaster-work sometimes merits being picked out in several colours. In the London drawing room of an Edwardian flat belonging to Helen, Lady Dashwood, I painted the walls matt daffodil and picked out the mouldings in gloss white. For the Duke of Abercorn's rotunda, I used deep primrose yellow behind the palest lettuce-green scagliola columns and below a coffered ceiling decorated in three greys.

Far left In my country house, I wanted a simple background in the drawing room, on which to display pictures and objects. I stretched rose pink cotton on the walls and made large draped curtains to frame the window. The carpet is one of my geometric designs. Dried leaves and plants change with the seasons.

Right An elevation drawing of a guest bedroom in a duplex apartment in Cambridge, Massachusetts, showing the wall treatment for a seating area below a window. Wooden venetian blinds cover the window.

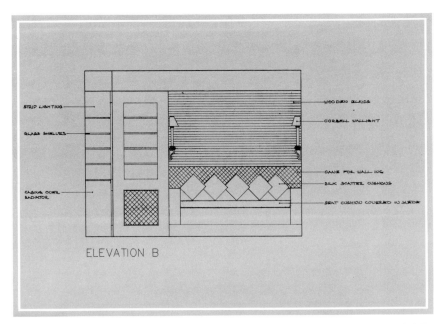

ELEVATION B

Below Raw timber is used to line the walls of my showroom, producing a warm, textured effect.

Never paint one wall a different colour from the rest. The result inevitably looks confused. The same advice applies to alcoves, unless the recess is enclosed by a handsome classical architrave which makes it worthy of this kind of attention.

The inherent scope of paint can be extended further by adopting special techniques such as dragging, ragging or stippling. Broadly speaking, these methods involve 'distressing' the painted surface while it is still wet, to create textural, patterned effects. A simpler alternative is to apply the colour brokenly at the outset, using tools such as sponges, rags or stiff brushes, which leave characteristic imprints. A sense of depth is achieved by applying a number of contrasting or toning colours. Some techniques, such as marbling, are designed to simulate real materials, but these require a high degree of skill to be effective.

Paint effects involving broken colour have become increasingly prevalent in recent years, so much so that I believe their popularity is already waning. Because they are relatively easy and inexpensive to execute many people have become over-enthusiastic, decorating everything in sight. It must be remembered that such a treatment looks best if it is used sparingly, relieved by plain neighbouring rooms. Most of the effects are insistent and the result can easily become overpowering if not handled with care.

Paint effects are not new. There are many examples of marbled or stippled rooms in late-seventeenth-century and eighteenth-century English houses, and simulations of stone or marble were popular when the real materials were hard to obtain or prohibitively expensive. One of the few places where I have used such a paint technique was in the bathroom of my former country house. Here I applied black on white panelling with a sponge, to give the appearance of granite, with the surrounds painted beige and white. I based this idea on a treatment I had seen in the Winterthur Museum in Delaware, which houses a collection of early Americana.

Paper

Wallpaper generates an atmosphere of cosiness and intimacy and can be very appealing in country living rooms and bedrooms. It is also useful for disguising awkward corners, hiding pipe cases and generally lending coherence to a badly proportioned area, such as a rambling passageway.

Although most people think of pattern when they think of wallpaper, interesting textural versions are also available in plain colours, although not those designed to simulate brick, stone, rough plaster or wood. There is no place for such a treatment in the home.

Many papers are available in ranges which are coordinated with furnishing fabrics and matching borders or friezes. In rooms that lack architectural detail, these can be very effective. I once papered an

entrance hall in a stippled ochre design and added banding of bronze brown where the walls met the ceiling and skirting boards, as well as around the doors and windows and vertically in the corners.

Wallpaper can also look very striking when varnished. In bathrooms it must be waterproofed or sealed for protection.

Fabric

Fabric-covered walls are very luxurious and very feminine. The material you use must not be too thick – cotton, linen twill and silk are all suitable. I have also used tweed, camelhair and, more economically, hessian. In my library in the country there is only one portion of wall – over the fireplace – without shelves. I covered this with rust-red silk velvet – in fact, my grandmother's evening skirt.

Fabric always adds great textural interest. Even the plainest cotton has a softness impossible to achieve with matt paint, whereas hessian has a nubbly surface which works well in a tailored, modern room.

There are several methods of applying fabric to walls. The simplest is to buy fabric that is already paper-backed and can be stuck in place like wallpaper. You can also construct flush panels and wrap these in fabric before securing them to the wall. Stretching fabric ('walling') involves battening around the perimeter of the wall, interlining between the battens and then pulling the fabric flat by nailing from the centre out to the edges. The nails or staples can then be covered with braid, petersham ribbon, a strip of gilt wood or a band of the same fabric. The richest way to use fabric, however, is to gather or pleat it. Because this uses so much material and involves a high degree of skill to execute, it is a very expensive way to decorate.

Never cover the walls of a dining room with fabric – it will retain the smell of food and cigars. In the eighteenth century, when Robert Adam designed the state dining room at Syon Park, the seat of the Duke of Northumberland, elaborate shutters were introduced to lend decorative interest in the absence of fabric at the windows.

Panelling

Panelling, perhaps because it is expensive, seems to give people a sense of security. Again, the range of treatments is broad: wood panels can be polished or matt, painted or lacquered. Pine panelling can look charming unpolished and with a scrubbed finish, but I prefer it to be painted, as it was historically. The vogue for stripped pine has exposed much inferior wood and carpentry that was originally intended to be filled and decorated.

Better quality wood, however, does not need to be covered. I have recently used a lot of flush sycamore panelling with contrasting banding in oak or ash. Polished mahogany panelling can also look very effective in a library, office or boardroom, especially set off with an ebonized

Far left At the top of this staircase, I hung a four panelled eighteenth-century leather screen and massed chrysanthemums in front of them on a table already in the client's possession.

inset band. Inlaid brass can be used to trim panels as well – either three narrow strips or a single wide one.

The effect of panelling without the expense can be created using a number of techniques. To add style to a plain little room I once adapted an idea I had seen in one of the durbar rooms in the city palace in Jaipur. I created panels in a peach colour and then bordered each one with a broad white band, inscribed with four parallel black lines, set equally apart. For a dining room in Paris, I created another panelled effect by using five different marblized bookend papers.

Below This stylish London kitchen in black, white and grey displays a careful integration of built-in units and appliances. The wall tiling extends right up to the ceiling, giving a crisp, neat look.

Tiling

Wall tiles are a practical choice for the functional areas of the home, such as kitchens and bathrooms. They last much longer than a paint finish and are waterproof and easy to keep clean. Today, tiles come in an incredible variety of colours and designs – ones that suit any decorative scheme.

It is important to tile the whole wall, not just a portion of it. Tiling which starts at the bath, for example, and finishes three-quarters of the wall up the wall, looks mean and ill-proportioned. Similarly, in a kitchen extend the tiling all the way to the ceiling. I favour plain designs with an inset or flanking border. I sometimes simply add two horizontal lines in a contrasting colour, one tile down from the ceiling and one tile up from the worksurface.

In the bathroom, care should be taken over the joint between the bathtub and wall surface. Because the bath will expand and contract with changes in temperature, coving tiles applied to the perimeter invariably come away. The best solution I have seen for the problem was a precast fibreglass bath incorporating a lip around the edge.

OTHER SURFACES

In a typical interior there are a number of other surfaces which offer the opportunity to use interesting materials.

Many homes have some built-in cupboard space – wardrobes in bedrooms, hall closets, alcove cupboards in living rooms or studies. Few are attractive enough in their own right to stand out as a feature. Doors can be panelled, louvred or made of trellis to give more interest. On the whole, however, I prefer flush doors decorated to match the rest of the room so that the cupboard becomes almost invisible. If the walls are papered this can be extended across the cupboard doors. Make sure the paper is wrapped around the thickness of the leading edge so that it doesn't pull away. For the ultimate in disguise, the cupboard can be constructed so that it starts above the skirting board and ends just beneath the cornice. Pictures or engravings can be hung on the doors, securely fixed through from the back. I have even made wardrobes out of panelled six-leaved screens, floor to ceiling, covered in fabric and set across the corner of a room, with panels formed by polished brass nails.

In kitchens, built-in plastic laminate counters are hard to better for practicality. Choice of colour is important. Avoid vivid primaries which do not enhance the appearance of food and of which you will quickly tire.

Vanity units in bathrooms can have tops of scrubbed oak, varnished mahogany, formica, polished granite, marble or lacquered wood. The wash-basin must be fixed under the level of the top, not sitting on it. The side of the bathtub can be panelled or decorated to match the walls.

CHAPTER SIX

SOFT FURNISHING

Fabric dresses a room. Even in a warm climate, an interior finished entirely in hard materials would be an ungiving, unyielding place. Soft furnishing – that is, curtains, blinds, upholstery and bed- and table-linen – alleviates the crisp lines of internal architecture and promotes an atmosphere of comfort.

But there are also practical advantages. Fabric adds to the physical warmth of a room, as well as insulating against noise. At the window, it filters light, provides privacy and blocks draughts; as a cover for furniture it is easy to maintain and economical to replace.

For the interior designer, fabric is an important source of colour, texture and pattern. My delight in the qualities of different fabrics dates back to my childhood when my mother and I were involved in her elaborate amateur production of The Lady with the Lamp. *One day our costumes arrived from the local dressmaker – a rich velvet coat, a rustling silk crinoline. The excitement of the contrasts in colour and texture remain a vivid memory.*

Fabric can express any style you choose for your interior. It can be majestically draped and swagged; neatly tailored and trimmed; simply gathered in loose folds. The art of successful soft furnishing is, in fact, not unlike the art of dressmaking.

iron
armatures

striped chintzes
or geometric cottons
could be used instead
of overused stock "passmenterie".
DH Dec 86.

freely adapted from
J.J.Lequeu's
drawings c.1792

USING FABRICS

The great furnishing fabrics of the past were silk damask and velvet. Although such luxury is largely unknown today, we have instead a richer range of materials from which to choose, both natural and synthetic, and in every conceivable pattern, colour and texture.

During my career I have established certain preferences. I abhor cotton satin, especially the printed variety. I like wool, tweed, jute, linen, poplin, unglazed cotton, glazed chintz and silk velvet. I used to dislike synthetic materials, but I have come to accept that mixing man-made fibres with natural ones increases performance. There are even some completely synthetic structures that can be woven attractively.

Different types of fabric naturally suit different locations and uses. In the living and dining rooms, for example, a traditional choice would be woven damask. The plain cotton variety dyes well; the silk and cotton mixture is most attractive. With this I would use a heavy textured plain fabric, such as wool or linen, with small patterns to cover chairs and sofas. In such a context, an interesting addition would be Siamese silk cushion covers. I would reserve crisp, cleanly printed chintz for bedrooms.

As always, however, bending or breaking rules can result in striking and original solutions. I often use tweed, occasionally flannel and even plain cotton ticking. Once, for a fashion showroom, I upholstered armchairs in one of the overcoat materials produced by the company. Curtains made of dress fabric can be striking and inexpensive, but they will not last long.

I find that the most exciting way to use fabrics is to contrast different textures in the same room. I relish glazed chintz next to rough tweed, paper silk taffeta with chamois leather, printed heavy linen with silk velvet. Recently I designed an all-white bedroom using three different white cotton weaves: a plain even-weave cotton, one woven with a small denim chevron and a heavy twill. The walls were whitewashed, the flooring white cord carpet, the pictures black and white drawings and the objects all different whites, creating a series of subtle contrasts that was very pleasing.

Many furnishing fabrics are produced today in coordinated ranges that enable you to curtain a window, drape a bed or table and cover an armchair using the same basic pattern, appropriately scaled. Such simple coordination can be very effective, creating an intimate, enclosed atmosphere particularly suitable for bedrooms or dressing rooms. But try not to over-upholster. Fabric walls, covered tables, elaborate draperies and a tented ceiling would be too much.

DESIGNING FABRICS

My first fabric design was a small, formalized daisy, interspersed with a diamond. The repeat was only one inch across and, at that time, the early 1960s, it was difficult to find anyone who could print such a small pattern. The fabric was produced for my own house, but when clients saw it, demand grew and I decided to design more.

Soon after, a fabric wholesaler in New York asked me to make a collection. The result was a range of geometric designs printed in the United States on heavy linens, fine cottons and ribbed silk. These were marketed alongside a wallpaper collection of matching prints and colour-ways. Since then I have designed and selected a number of collections, many of which are still in production. I draw much inspiration from antique fabrics – visiting old mills and museums is exciting and stimulating.

Once on holiday in the South of France I visited Soleido in Tarascon, where the traditional Provençal flower patterns originated. One of the company's directors spotted me in the showroom and immediately took me upstairs to the attic to show me the old Directoire printing blocks. We chose which ones we would reprint, and this became my Tarascon collection.

Many of my designs, like the patterns I have created for carpets, are geometric, but I am currently bringing out formal flower patterns in a new collection of woven and printed fabrics.

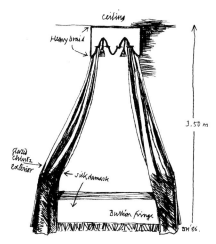

WINDOW TREATMENTS

Window dressing can vary from a neat white holland blind to the most extravagantly rich drapery in heavy woven silk damask. Whatever the style, however, the purpose of covering a window is to filter or screen light, maintain privacy at night, insulate the room against heat loss and sound, and soften the bare outline of the opening itself.

Curtains

I prefer curtains to be lined and interlined. This gives a feeling of quality, makes the curtains last longer and hang better, and increases insulation. In bedrooms I also add black lining to block out the light completely.

Curtains made of muslin, linen, canvas or silk taffeta can be left unlined, however, since the point of using such fabrics is to appreciate their texture. One of the most striking examples of such a treatment I have ever seen was in a Paris apartment, where the curtains were composed of five layers of fine tulle, each one a different colour.

Curtain styles vary widely. There are, however, certain guidelines which you should adhere to. In general, curtains should look generous and always extend to the floor. Curtains that end at the window sill – or worse, at an indeterminate length beneath it – look mean and do not display the fabric to best advantage. If you do not want floor-length curtains, opt for a blind instead or café curtains, which hang from halfway up the window, covering the lower portion down to the sill. These should usually be combined with full-length outer curtains.

There is, conversely, a vogue for trailing curtains on the floor. A

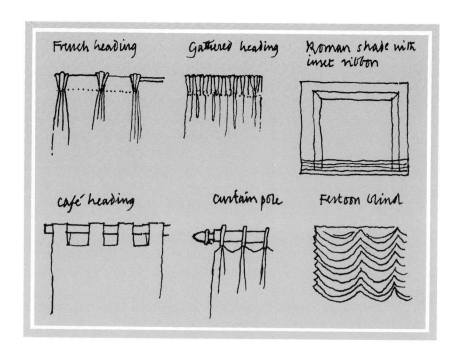

Right Walls, blinds, tablecloth and bedcover in this Chelsea bedroom were all made of the same fabric, a fresh and cheerful print still produced by my company. The plain curtains, carpet and upholstery provide visual relief from the patterned surfaces.

sweep of fine material which is allowed to fan out rather like the base of a bustle can look sculptural and feminine, but the effect must not be overdone. Heavy fabric bunched in an untidy heap simply looks absurd.

Unless the room imposes a particular period style, curtains should be as simple as possible. In an eighteenth-century drawing room, for example, nothing could be more enjoyable than a swagged drapery. In most situations, however, the neat, elegant lines of modern headings are appropriate. Of the many different curtain styles, I seem to favour four treatments: pencil pleats, French pleats, a gathered heading using a brass pole and rings, and festoon curtains.

Festoon curtains are enjoying a tremendous popularity. These have a standard heading, but do not draw back; instead, they are reefed on cords so that the fabric can be ruched up in loops. I have used festoon curtains with great success, particularly in period rooms but, as always, when an idea becomes too popular, it is best to avoid it for a while, until some of its original freshness returns.

A straightforward, standard solution may not be possible in some locations. For a semi-circular nursery window, for example, I devised curtains which fit right round the curve and drew up like theatre curtains. If a pair of windows are very close together, I always endeavour to leave a margin of wall between – I dislike curtains which cover an entire wall. In other cases, I have used dress curtains – those which do not close but soften the room – and combined these with a blind to screen the light. In a New York hotel suite, where the night-time view was spectacular, I kept the curtains permanently joined at the top, and held them back lower down with tie-backs, to give a degree of privacy without losing the view. If curtains do not need to be drawn, you can fix the curtain hooks into screw eyes sunk into the window frame and do without a track altogether. If they are to be drawn, always use a cord-controlled track to avoid soiling the fabric.

Decorative trimming

Many curtains benefit from being trimmed in some way. This does not mean fussy fringes or tasselled cords, but neat, tailored details that provide a sympathetic finishing touch.

Pelmets can introduce a charming note of whimsy to an otherwise plain room. These are particularly effective in bedrooms and dining rooms, or wherever architectural detail is lacking. Pelmets can either be flat and shaped, or gathered and fixed to a pelmet board. Whatever their design, they must be fairly deep – never less than ten inches. For a really large window, they can extend as far down as forty-eight inches.

The prime function of a pelmet is to give curtains a finished look by covering the heading. But they can also be used to adjust the propor-tions of a room. If the room lacks height, the pelmet and drapery can be taken up above the window to cover the 'dead light' – in other words,

straight pelmet with gathered frill.

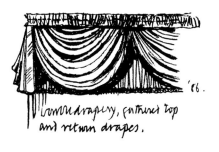

loosen drapery, gathered top and return drapes.

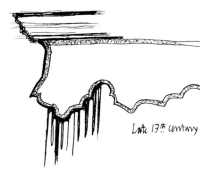

Late 17th century

simple drapery for single bed against the wall.

Far right In an Irish room containing a pair of single brass beds, I arranged them opposite each other, against either wall. The simple draped effect was created by arranging a length of Laura Ashley fabric over an armature projecting from the wall. The fabric is lined with another print which matches the bedhead, bedcover and valance.

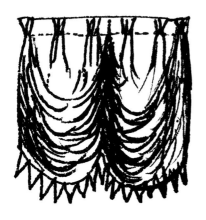

Curtain treatment for Bridgewater minimum layout DX.

the spare margin of wall between the top of the window and the ceiling.

Inspiration for the shape of the pelmet can be taken from historical sources, such as conversation-piece pictures. Surprisingly, Victorian railway-station canopies are another good source of ideas. I have even based the design of a pelmet on a nineteenth-century balustrade.

Other decorative touches can be introduced by banding curtains and pelmets in contrasting colours or fabrics, or in petersham ribbon. This can run along the edge or be inset. If tie-backs are required, I prefer fabric ones, made of the same material as the curtain and trimmed in the same way. Again, these must be generously proportioned, not narrow little strips.

Blinds

Used on their own, blinds are effective and attractive in situations where floor-length curtains would be impractical or even unsafe – in a kitchen, for example. Their crisp, linear style also suits offices and modern interiors, but combined with curtains and trimmed appropriately they can also enhance more traditional rooms. To filter light or if privacy is required, blinds are infinitely preferable to net curtains.

The basic type of blind is the simple holland blind which operates on a roller. These can also be fixed at the sill and pulled up, the cord being fed through two screw eyes on the soffit and back down to the sill. Roller blinds can be inexpensively made by laminating thin material to the basic holland blind fabric.

Roman shades, which pull up vertically in folds, are another useful solution. Trimmed with contrasting or toning bands, they can look elegant enough for use in a living room. The bands can be inset vertical stripes, used to form panels or run along the edge. For a large floor-to-ceiling picture window I once used ten six-inch-pleat Roman shades in ochre, trimmed with brown and red braid.

Blinds are available in other materials apart from fabric. Both wooden and aluminium Venetian blinds come in many different colours and thicknesses. If you like the flexibility of Venetian blinds, but want to avoid their rather clinical look, pinoleum blinds, made of split bamboo, can be very attractive. These can also be painted to match the decoration.

For other ways to screen windows, see page 98.

BED-HANGINGS

Draped and canopied beds have been a feature of grand houses from the earliest times. In the days when houses consisted of a series of inter-connecting chambers without halls or passageways, bed drapery was an important way of providing privacy. Of course, it also served as protection against the cold. Today, although these functions are largely irrelevant, the tester bed remains popular. As well as immediately introducing a strong note of style, it gives a reassuring feeling of warmth and protection.

Right For a small Park Lane bedroom, I covered the walls in lettuce green moiré and fixed floral prints on the jibbed wardrobe doors. Over the bed, I hung a green and white geometric fabric of my design to give the room a sense of importance.

Below In Oman, I created a guest suite using a cool colour-way of 'Wolfsgarten', one of my fabric designs based on a German document. The imposing tester bed suits the scale of the room.

Look at medieval beds – for an early house.

Left A simply tailored tester bed, with a plain outer pelmet and pleated inner pelmet. Contrast banding on the outer pelmet and leading edges of the bed drapery matches the lining.

A tester is, properly speaking, the canopy over a freestanding four-poster bed. You can buy an antique or reproduction bed of this design and drape it accordingly, but there are other, less expensive ways of achieving the same effect.

One is to construct a lightweight frame, attach pelmets and bolt the entire canopy to the ceiling. The drapery is simply suspended from it: a floor-length curtain behind the bedhead, and one at each corner. In 1957, when I was redesigning my own bedroom, I wanted the look of a four-poster bed but could not afford an antique one. I constructed a tester using the method I have just described, with brown and black glazed chintz on the exterior, and a beige cotton lining. Curiously enough, I still have the same bed today. Though now it is only a half-tester, it has seen six successive bedrooms and the chintz has worn well, which demonstrates that if you buy the right fabric in the first place it will last. I have since designed many other tester beds for clients all over the world, from Miami to Melbourne.

Variations on the same theme include half-testers, coronas and half-coronas. The half-tester consists of a canopy fixed to the ceiling which extends only a couple of feet over the bed, with a curtain at either side. Coronas are oval-shaped canopies; half-coronas are semi-circular canopies, where the material is draped out wide to left and right and held in place with tie-backs.

An even simpler arrangement is to fix a pole to the wall, so that it projects over the bed, and drape fabric over it. If there is an alcove, the bed can also be set back into it and the entire recess curtained.

When draping a bed, an important point to remember is that it must look as effective from the inside as it does externally. This means that everything – pelmets, canopy and curtains – must be lined and finished attractively. The interior can be the same as the exterior, or lined in a contrasting fabric. Sun-ray pleating on the underside of the canopy is luxurious. Although the curtains need not draw, they must be generous and full; they can be tied back or simply hang straight. Pelmets can be simple and straight, or more extravagantly crenellated or draped.

Bed-linen should also be carefully coordinated with the drapery. The bedhead should be covered in one of the fabrics used for the hangings. Ideally, this should be a loose cover that can be removed for cleaning. The same fabric can be used to make a full-length bedspread, or to face the top side of an eiderdown.

TABLE-LINEN

Table-linens are another source of pattern, texture and colour. In a dining room, I often make an inexpensive table from plywood or blockboard and keep it permanently covered with a floor-length cloth. Then on top of that I put another cloth in the same material, or a different design but colour-coordinated, which can be removed and washed; between the two you can insert a sheet of plastic to prevent

Far left For a main bedroom in an apartment on Fifth Avenue in New York, I devised a simple white tweed tester bed, one of the first to be made in the United States since the turn of the century. The quilted bedspread is white chintz and even the carpet is white.

spills penetrating. This is the solution I have adopted in my own London apartment. For a circular plywood table in the living room, which must be used for dining, and which also hides the television, I have two different cloths: a coral-red cotton and a cherry, aubergine and white formal cotton print. These go on top of an antique Indian cloth of liver brown. I then vary the table settings and flower arrangements to suit the particular cloth. The bottom tablecloth should always extend to the ground, except in the case of restaurant tables, where this can prove inconvenient.

Tablecloths, however, do not just belong in the dining room. I often cover side tables in living rooms, bathrooms and bedrooms with floor-length cloths, especially if the table is uninteresting in design: this lends an air of solidity. Small square, circular or triangular tables look particularly attractive covered in this way. The cover can hang in folds or be cut and tailored like an altar-cloth. As well as furnishing fabric, I have used quilting, antique fabrics, felt and tweed. In an Australian department store, I covered a table with a rather ordinary Persian carpet, assembled a collection of pewter on top and achieved echoes of Vermeer.

UPHOLSTERY

There are two basic types of upholstery: tight or close covering, and loose covers. Certain styles of furniture can only be tight-covered; others can be treated successfully either way.

Tight covering looks neat and tailored and preserves the lines of the piece. Most antique chairs and many sofas demand close covering. Particular attention must be paid to the edges, finishing off with braid or brass nails. The fabric can be sprayed with a proprietary protection which helps maintenance, although I often find that marks can easily be removed by rubbing the spot with a crust of bread, the crumbs acting like an india rubber.

Loose covers are more informal and can be removed easily, either for cleaning or to change the colour scheme. It is also cheaper to have loose covers made for a sofa or chairs than to have them re-upholstered. For furniture that can take it, it is often a good idea to upholster in a dark material for the winter months, then add light covers for the summer to brighten up the room. And even simpler seasonal changes can be accomplished by changing the covers of scatter cushions.

An interesting textured fabric can be a good choice for upholstering antiques. A grey-brown slub weave used to cover a Louis XVI chair, for example, would both enhance the piece and help it to blend in with more modern pieces. There is no need to recover antiques strictly in period.

Far right A small London bathroom was given character by applying striped glazed chintz to the walls. The same fabric was then used to make a blind for the window and to cover the front of the bath and washbasin.

Shavers only

Above right A country-house bedroom, redecorated in the 1970s, shows the use of elaborate window and bed-drapery in keeping with the grandeur of the setting. A half-corona frames the bedhead, while the window is formally dressed in the same fabric.

Below right The view from the window in my country drawing room – a vista I created with hornbeams and a lawn. The window, built in 1820, has elaborate drapery – tails and a skirted treatment – to give interest and drama to an otherwise plain but tall room. The curtains are made of simple French cotton, the same material being used to cover the walls.

Far right The bedroom in my London apartment has a tester bed in the middle of the room, reflected in the mirror in the drawing room. The walls are distempered. The silk-damask interior lining of the bed is identical in colour to the glazed chintz used for the external drapery.

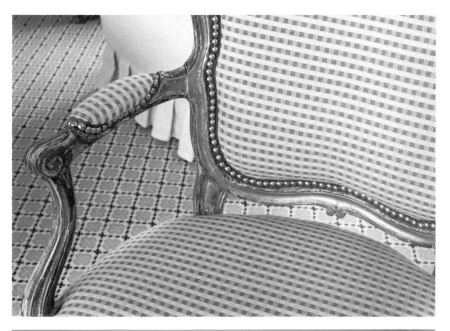

Right On a set of fine eighteenth-century elbow chairs I used a small jacquard weave of my own design. I trimmed the chairs with bright brass nails over a petersham ribbon in a contrasting colour.

Below right This children's room in a London apartment shows the use of coordinating fabric and paper to promote a feeling of warmth and comfort. The cheerful geometric print is fresh without being too dominating. Even the legs of the upholstered stool are covered in fabric.

Far right Bathrooms should be furnished, comfortable and welcoming places. Here the centrally positioned bathtub is encased in wooden panelling which matches the vanity-top. One of my geometric prints is used to skirt the wash-basin and cover the armless chair beside the bath; another to make a floor-length tablecloth.

CHAPTER SEVEN

ARRANGING ROOMS

The impression a room makes at first sight is largely conditioned by the furniture it contains and how this is arranged. Of these two factors, it is arrangement that is the most important. If pieces are positioned awkwardly the fact that they are the finest antiques will make no difference, the room will still look static and indifferent. It is not what *you own, but* how *you use it.*

Almost every room I have entered could have been better arranged; in friends' houses, I have often moved the furniture about to improve the appearance of a room. One evening, after shooting at Belvoir, I moved the Duke of Rutland, sleeping on a sofa, from one side of the room to the other, aided and abetted by the other house guests. On another occasion, I moved Lady Hesketh's very heavy sofa at Pomfret Lodge, and then had to spend some time hoovering – the cost, perhaps, of having such firm views about design.

Every interior designer should be familiar with the history of furniture and appreciate the inspiration the past has to offer. I bought my first antique at the age of fifteen. It was a Regency dining chair, in grained rosewood and gold leaf, and cost one pound: I still have it. This was the beginning of an interest in furniture and historical interiors that absorbs me still.

THE DEVELOPMENT OF THE FURNISHED INTERIOR

The history of furniture and interior decoration is a rich and complex subject, far more detailed than the brief summary which follows. My intention here is merely to introduce the essential characteristics of different periods and whet the appetite for more extensive research. The literature on the subject is vast, and visiting collections in museums and historic houses can also provide a stimulating illustration of the progression of designs and the different contexts in which they evolved.

Furniture is a comparatively modern development. Until the late Middle Ages, only royalty, the aristocracy and high-ranking churchmen possessed chairs; everyone else sat on stone or perhaps wooden benches, or on the floor.

The first European sofa is generally reckoned to be the Knole sofa, dated about 1612. This design, which is still being reproduced, has an upright back and cantilevered sides which can be let down. But there is little furniture of this period or earlier that is not in museum collections or public ownership.

It is not until later in the seventeenth century that furniture becomes generally usable for the modern interior designer. This period gives us tallboys – high chests of drawers on turned legs – square-backed armchairs and cabinets with intricate inlays. Oak was a favoured choice of wood for more everyday pieces.

By far the most popular and enduring period of furniture design was the eighteenth century. It was not called the Golden Age for nothing: all over Europe, sublimely attractive and interesting designs were produced, with subtle variations from country to country. The early part of the period gives us handsome, plain mahogany sideboards and solid but elegant wardrobes and chairs. The mid-eighteenth century, the time of Chippendale, represents the classic period of furniture-making: Gainsborough chairs with upholstered arms and mahogany frames, Serpentine chests of drawers and carved and gilded mirrors. The end of the century saw more refinement: elegant, oval-backed elbow chairs, oval mirror frames and marble-topped console tables.

Contemporary conversation-pieces, such as those by Hogarth and Devis, provide us with evidence of how furniture was used in the Georgian interior. Most rooms were under-furnished to the point of looking sparse, with pieces often pushed back against the walls, not grouped as in today's arrangements.

By the beginning of the nineteenth century – the Regency period – furniture had become more delicate and smaller in scale. Chairs were extremely refined; there were cupboards inlaid with brass-key patterns and Greek-tombstone-topped clothes presses. It was not uncommon to see Egyptian motifs – crocodiles and sphinxes – the result of contemporary interest in the Battle of the Nile.

Our picture of the intensely overcrowded historic interior dates from the Victorians. Such overcrowding was often the result of generations of inheritance, as family homes were sold and the contents assimilated or relatives passed on collections of chairs or porcelain.

But the Victorians also had a passion for clutter, so much so that it was not uncommon for some of the more important pieces of furniture to be stored in the attic to make way for more bric-à-brac, canework and one hundred and one different objects. Careers spent in far-flung corners of the Empire resulted in a plethora of exotic curios: elephant's-foot umbrella stands, brass gongs suspended on ivory tusks, vases filled with peacock feathers. As far as furniture was concerned, the Victorians prized comfort above aesthetics. Pieces were generally heavy, over-stuffed and fussily decorated. Many of the designs aped another period, but unsuccessfully.

The Edwardians continued in the same vein. Although some of the bric-à-brac was cleared away, there were heavy-handed historical pastiches – ill-proportioned Georgian-style dining chairs and panels decorated with over-serious interpretations of Renaissance carving.

The arrival of the machine age saw a radically different approach. In the 1920s and 1930s, inspired by the modern movement, a number of people were encouraged to change their attitude towards living. New homes were commissioned in town and the country and, in keeping with the streamlined architecture, the interiors made no reference to the past, either in material or design. Furniture in bold new shapes was produced in stainless steel and chrome, and upholstered in leather or heavy diagonal weaves. Rooms were sparse and functional, with minimal detailing, severe, dramatic lighting and an absence of super-fluous decoration.

At the same time, a less extreme reaction to the past was taking place. A number of interested people began to employ the newly emerged 'interior designers', such as Syrie Maugham and Elsie Mendel, to edit out the clutter of their family homes and achieve a relaxed, yet luxurious atmosphere, mixing modern materials with antique furniture. Almost no historic houses were given this treatment. In 1936, Winnafreda, Countess of Portarlington, transformed the gloomiest of Scottish fishing lodges into a lively and attractive interior by limeing the pitch-pine panelling and furnishing with 120 yards of cream satin and eighty yards of *tête de negre* carpet she had ordered from London by telegraph.

After the austerity of the Second World War, there was a welcome return to colour, wit and gaiety. Reproduction Regency furniture was much in vogue, its fine proportions particularly suited to the small scale of modern rooms. But this was also the time when families with inherited estates and possessions had to make momentous decisions about the long-term economic viability of their houses. Many larger properties were given up and many, to the cost of our heritage, were eventually demolished (1,000 in Britain alone). One effect of this drastic upheaval was that an enormous amount of period furniture

appeared on the market, transforming antique dealing from a specialized business to a booming international trade.

In the post-war years, one can see three distinct movements in interior design that are related to the choice and use of furniture. The first, and most popular, is the highly traditional look, originally developed by the English design firm Colefax and Fowler, and now widely imitated on both sides of the Atlantic. This approach makes no reference to the twentieth century, but relies on charming, stylized interpretations of period designs and decoration. It is, above all, highly English, and immensely feminine in its use of trimmings such as ribbons, fringes and bows.

The second is resolutely modern, and rejects any hint of the past, either in furniture or decoration. A variation on this theme is the approach of designers who work only within the context of what is currently in vogue – that is, modern in the sense of being 'in fashion'.

The third category consists of a mixture of old and new. This is the approach to which I have adhered throughout my career. I have chosen this method of working because I believe that the alternatives, as I see them, tend to be superimposed both on clients and their homes. My starting point, on the other hand, is always the clients' own tastes, possessions and needs, so that whatever design solution I propose develops and improves what is already there.

It is the combination of styles and periods which makes a satisfying and original interior. I like to see modern sculpture on an eighteenth-century commode, or eighteenth-century objects mounted on contemporary perspex cubes. To me, the historical purists who recreate a period look down to the last detail end up with a museum, not a home. Further, they are ignoring the fact that few historic houses date solely from one period; their contents were also disparate in age and style. Conversely, modernists, by cutting themselves off from the past, are depriving themselves of the richness and quality previous ages had to offer.

It is more difficult to blend different elements in an interior; it takes experiment, patience and inspiration. Generally, however, I have found that most antiques prior to the middle of the nineteenth century will mix well with contemporary furniture, whereas Victorian and Edwardian pieces will not. Antique chairs look very well covered in a plain modern weave. Coffee tables should always be contemporary in design – the coffee table only dates from about 1920, so 'antique' styles are an utter anachronism. Modern rooms can be given depth by displaying old objects, sculpture or pictures.

Today, magazines and home-furnishing catalogues emphasize 'total' looks, assembled rather like a kit, to provide instant atmosphere. The result is invariably as lifeless as a studio set. To achieve vitality in the interior, you must avoid prefabricated solutions.

Above far left With careful selection, old and new can be combined very effectively in a grouping of furniture. This conversation area juxtaposes a contemporary sofa and upholstered stool with a period chair.

Below far left This living room in a London apartment is large enough to contain three generous conversation areas. Breaking an expanse of space up in this way makes a better use of the available area and reduces it to more manageable proportions.

CHOOSING FURNITURE

You cannot choose a piece of furniture in isolation; it must serve a function within the layout you have planned for the room as a whole. However, it is always worth spending time investigating what is available so that whenever you make your choice, it is an informed one.

Good antiques are expensive, prohibitively so for many people. But if you can afford the outlay, it is worth remembering that antiques have never lost their financial status, quite apart from the aesthetic pleasure they can provide. And there is nothing to equal a fine piece of furniture from the seventeenth, eighteenth or early nineteenth century in terms of craftsmanship, materials and design.

My least favourite antiques are Victorian and Edwardian. Although there are some exceptions, most are too heavy and dominant for my taste, and none look well mixed with pieces from other periods. On the other hand, I have a particular liking for the forthright designs of the early eighteenth century and the neo-classical style of the 1820s.

Bargains can sometimes be found in junk shops and at auctions, but the better antique dealers are more likely to have pieces that are worthwhile as investments. An alternative, if you cannot afford an original piece, is to buy a good interpretation or reproduction. Look for the least pretentious, and avoid simulated antiques with faked wormholes and distressed finishes.

Contemporary furniture encompasses a broad range of styles. The classic, modern look first originated at the beginning of the modern movement in the 1920s, and displayed clean, functional lines and use of materials such as leather, chrome and stainless steel. Within the modern idiom, various interpretations have emerged at different times. Scandinavian furniture, in particular 'Danish Modern', enjoyed a vogue in the early 1960s. Much of this looks *passé* today, but certain pieces, such as Arne Jacobsen's Swan chair, have a more timeless quality.

Although I have made use of such furniture in the past, it is playing less and less of a role in my designs today. This is not to say that modern furniture has no merit. There are many excellent designers and craftsmen producing interesting interpretations which display both a high degree of skill and good quality materials. What should be avoided, however, are the gimmicky ideas which will look dated in a year.

Left Libraries should have an intimate atmosphere. Here, in my library in the country, walls are lined with books from floor to ceiling. Above the chimneypiece I stretched a piece of silk velvet from my grandmother's evening skirt.

Below The main staircase at Baron's Court, designed by William Vitruvius Morrison, is lit solely by a large skylight. Because the light in Ireland can be cold and grey, I decided to paint the walls a very warm scarlet. Halfway up the stairs, on the first landing, is a jib door – its brass handle is just visible on the left.

Previous page A drawing room in Park Lane has been symmetrically arranged but in such a was as to avoid a feeling of lifelessness. A good collection of architectural engravings surrounds the painting over the fireplace. The carpet is textured, and raw Indian silk has been used to cover the walls and for the curtains.

Left I devised this pale, luminous colour scheme for clients in North London who collect delightful drawings. The furniture arrangement is another variation on a symmetrical layout, making the best use of the available space.

Above At the end of a living room/gallery natural light filters through tall windows. The room is painted in three shades of beige; the curtains are one of my designs in white and beige; and a pair of blue sofas and four elbow chairs are grouped around a Louis XV chimneypiece.

Above A view of my London drawing room, looking from the bedroom. Decorative oval picture frames lit by individual picture lights and a smokeless-fuel fire create a glowing atmosphere to match the warmth of the colour scheme.

Right In this well-proportioned living room, two generous sofas to the left and right of the fireplace work well flanked by three elbow chairs. Opposite the fireplace, a large armless sofa provides a third seating area.

Previous page The magnificent dining room at Broadlands has four full-length van Dyck portraits. For my nephew and niece, I suggested a colour scheme of daffodil yellow for the walls and deep Naples yellow for the background of the frieze, the details of which were then picked out in pure white. The carpet I devised for this room reflects the classical motifs on the ceiling, which was designed by Henry Holland.

Left In my country dining room the eau de nil colour scheme is complemented by the pinkish patterned tablecloth. The table is set with individual flower arrangements – ramekins filled with primroses. The room is kept deliberately free of extraneous furniture.

Below The dining area of this London apartment has an English crystal chandelier hung low over the table and lit with tall candles. On the wall behind are a pair of early-eighteenth-century carved gold and white oval mirrors. The dining table, which seats six to eight, is covered with a patterned tablecloth. Chairs upholstered in Naples yellow make a pleasing contrast to the Venetian red of the fabric-covered walls.

Right My country bedroom includes a bath placed in an alcove, a small library, and a wash-basin under a window, set into the top of a bookcase. The books are all bound in vellum, beige or canvas which tone with the decorative scheme.

Below and far right His-and-her bathrooms in a London apartment are similarly laid out and furnished with memorabilia and engravings, but the atmosphere of each is quite different. The masculine version is severely tailored in dark colours; the feminine version is altogether lighter with its soft pink walls.

DESIGNING FURNITURE

When designing furniture I often take a traditional idea and update it. Inspiration can come from an antique seen in a shop, museum or auction; I always have a notepad with me so I can sketch details. Once the sketch has been formally drawn up by my furniture designers, a prototype is then constructed. This will be used for a time to see how it works, and modifications then carried out if necessary. Only after this process will the piece become part of our range.

Exploiting the qualities of different materials adds to the enjoyment of furniture. I often use interesting combinations of wood, metal, marble and scrubbed stone. For a sideboard, I may make the base of painted wood and build a hot plate flush into a granite top. Sidetables may have stone tops, too, in granite or marble, and I often use ash, sycamore, oak, walnut and beech for chairs, tables and cupboards.

Far left In our former country house, Britwell Salome, I placed my wife's bath in the middle of the room and the wash-basin in a panelled alcove. The crystal chandelier, gilt mirror, carpeting and a fabulous view of the Chilterns made a luxurious room in which bathing was a true pleasure.

Below Office furnishings must be practical but there is no reason why they should not be as comfortable and attractive as the furniture one lives with, as this desk design shows.

Right I often use traditional French chairs, produced in plain unvarnished ash or with a matt-paint finish. A good model from another period retains its honesty if the materials are simple, but never if they are faked to look antique.

Far right A classically inspired table and a bookcase produced as part of our range.

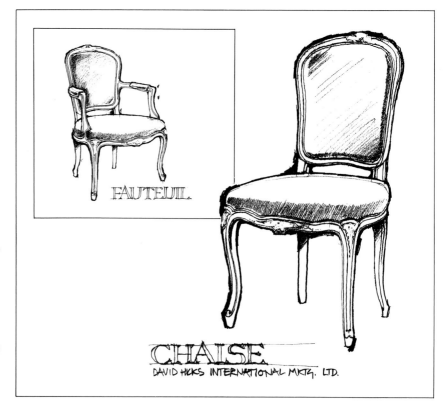

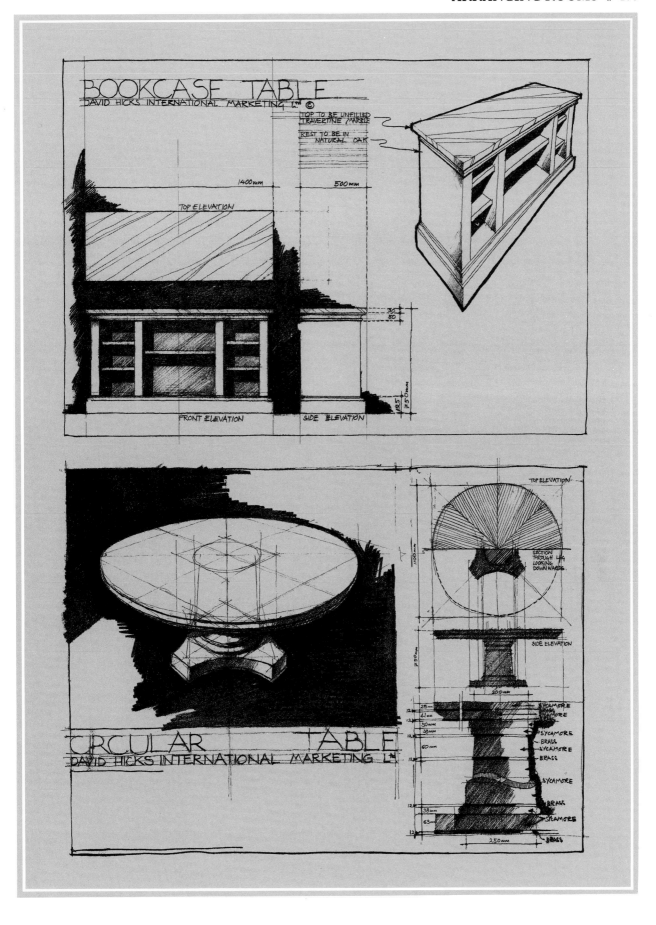

BOOKCASE TABLE
DAVID HICKS INTERNATIONAL MARKETING Lᵀᴰ ©

TOP TO BE UNFILLED TRAVERTINE /MARBLE

REST TO BE IN NATURAL OAK

1400mm   500mm

TOP ELEVATION

FRONT ELEVATION   SIDE ELEVATION

CIRCULAR   TABLE
DAVID HICKS INTERNATIONAL MARKETING Lᵀᴰ

TOP ELEVATION

SECTION THROUGH LEG LOOKING DOWNWARDS.

SIDE ELEVATION

SYCAMORE
BRASS
SYCAMORE
SYCAMORE
BRASS
SYCAMORE
BRASS

SYCAMORE

BRASS

SYCAMORE

BRASS

250mm

MAKING A FURNITURE LAYOUT

The purpose of arranging furniture is to achieve the maximum potential of a given space, both practically and aesthetically. Time spent during the planning stage, devising room layouts and investigating different solutions, will prevent you from making expensive and all too visible mistakes. Impulse buying should always be tempered by reason, particularly where furniture is concerned.

I derive enormous pleasure from playing with furniture layouts. Most of the alternatives can be plotted on paper; later it may be necessary to move pieces about physically to see if the arrangement can be improved upon.

Start by taking measurements of the furniture you own and the pieces you intend to buy. Using squared or graph paper, draw the shapes to scale, cut them out and place them on a plan of the area in question which has been made to the same scale. Juggle the pieces about, trying out different arrangements. Remember to allow clearance for drawers and cabinet doors and take into account leg room, ease of access and traffic. If you find it difficult to visualize layouts in miniature, you can always cut the furniture out full size from inexpensive brown paper and set the pieces out right on the floor.

In general, it is easier to plan the layout of a small room than a large one, chiefly because there are fewer visible alternatives. Larger spaces, particularly open-plan areas, are notoriously difficult to get right. Many people forget that a really big room cannot be treated as a scaled-up version of a smaller one: it is, in fact, more akin to a series of rooms, where each area must be related in a harmonious whole.

After you have arrived at what seems to be the correct solution, and put it into practice, some minor adjustments may be necessary. Once these have been accomplished, and the room works as it should, there should be no need for further alterations. It is true that some rooms can take a number of different layouts but, more usually, only one arrangement really is effective and you should resist the temptation for further change.

Living rooms

Whatever its size, the living room needs to provide the maximum amount of comfortable seating and display a definite sense of style. At the same time, it must not look crowded; one or two pieces that are not strictly functional can be tolerated, but not more.

You should first establish a genuine focal point. Many living rooms are arranged so that the eye is inevitably drawn to the television. It is far better to plan the layout around a more traditional centre of attention, such as the fireplace.

In most living rooms, the fireplace makes a natural focus for seating arrangements. Open fires produce a wonderful atmosphere; when the fire is not lit, the decorative surround can still provide a great deal of architectural interest. Broadly speaking, the two most popular styles of fireplace are English and French; the actual detailing of the surround, the chimney-piece and shelf, varies widely from period to period and according to the grandeur of its setting. Good reproductions or salvaged originals are easily available if the fireplace is missing, but you need not match the style exactly with the age of the house. On occasions, I have made a 'dummy' fireplace with an antique surround when the room needed a focal point. Nowadays, gas log fires are sensitively designed and are perfectly acceptable alternatives to an open fire.

Avoid grouping furniture so that a view is the centre of attention; at night, when the living room tends to be most used, the window will probably be curtained or screened.

Once you have decided on a focal point, you can devise a seating plan. If the living room is large, it may be necessary to have two conversation areas to break up the space. There is nothing wrong with the traditional three-piece suite, but the arrangement is so overworked that it is better to try a fresher approach. I much prefer a sofa facing two armchairs; but two sofas facing each other, with four elbow chairs, are ideal. Remember that two wing chairs never look right side by side; elbow or low-backed chairs do. And sofas should always have two, not three, seat cushions, however long they are. At all costs, avoid the mundane

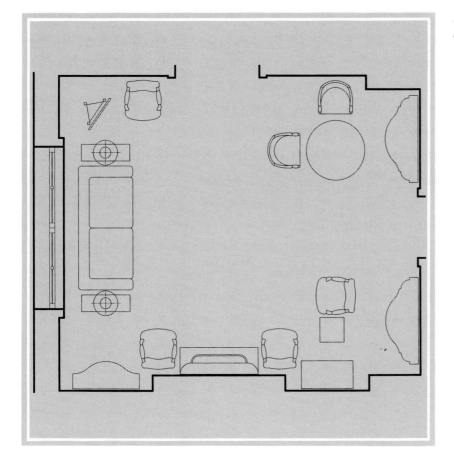

Left Furniture layout for a square living room, showing an ideal seating plan.

scheme of placing the sofa in front of the fire, flanked by two chairs. This creates a two-fold problem: it blocks the heat and access to the fireplace, and displays an uninteresting back view.

Seating areas should be accessorized with tables, which carry lights, drinks, ashtrays, objects and flower arrangements. A large upholstered stool in the centre of a layout for extra seating or magazines can give a welcoming, lived-in look.

Many living rooms often have to accommodate other activities apart from relaxation. Built-in storage can be very useful for concealing the evidence of these pursuits. A permanent home for a desk should be made away from the main seating area, in an alcove or corner. If you can spare a separate room to use as a library or study, make it comfortable with a couple of armchairs. The desk should be parallel or at right angles to the main window.

The advent of television has produced a particularly awkward element in the living room. There is nothing worse than seating grouped around a blank screen, particularly if it is perched on one of those ugly stands. The television must be placed where it is easily viewed, yet unobtrusive when not switched on. Solutions include installing the set in a bookcase, alcove or on a specially constructed podium with a cabinet to hide the working parts. But the arrangement I prefer is to place the television on the floor under a wide or circular table covered with a floor-length cloth. When it is needed, the cloth can be pulled up and the set viewed just as effectively as one might watch a play from the dress circle. Another alternative, particularly in a modern interior, is to accept the electronic gadgetry and display a well-designed, aggressive set as a feature in its own right. It can be placed on a trolley, together with stereo or video equipment, and wheeled in and out of sight as required.

Dining rooms

Relative to the other areas in the home, dining rooms should be under-furnished. The focal point will be, naturally enough, the dining table, but aside from chairs and serving tables, the room need contain little else but pictures.

Circular dining tables suit most rooms. More people can be fitted around them than around a rectangular table, and they also look softer. In a long room, an oval table would be a good solution. To cater for parties, a larger plywood top can be constructed and simply placed over the table so more people can be seated. Chairs should be ranged against the walls when they are not in use.

The practicality of the dining room can be improved by installing a serving hatch connecting it with the kitchen. This should be concealed and positioned near the serving table or sideboard. Every dining room could also benefit from having a sideboard with a hot plate built into the top.

Bedrooms

Most bedrooms need a good deal of built-in cupboard space to minimize clutter. This may well decrease the size of the room, but avoids the awkward shapes created by more traditional storage furniture, such as wardrobes and chests of drawers. For this reason I don't favour bedroom suites: coherence can be more effectively achieved by coordinating fabrics and linen (see page 134).

The bed is the dominant feature in the bedroom layout. A large double bed – perhaps a tester with draperies – can look attractive and dramatic in the centre of the room. Two single beds, on the other hand, often look stylish set longways against facing walls. The most common arrangement, however, is to place the bed so that the head is against one wall, with room for tables on either side. Even a single bed needs two bedside tables, for the sake of style and symmetry as much as practicality. These need not be elaborate, and can be made out of plywood and covered to the ground with fabric.

Dressing tables can look cumbersome and untidy, but there are designs which perform well without detracting from the appearance of the room. They must be placed to gain maximum benefit from daylight.

To give bedrooms a furnished look, it is essential to have at least one comfortable chair; a pair is ideal. If the room is large enough, a sofa flanked by two chairs will give a pleasing, boudoir atmosphere.

Extra seating and storage can be provided by a chest placed at the end of the bed, or an ottoman covered in fabric. This can also be a convenient place for the television to stand.

Kitchens

Although the kitchen layout is principally defined by the arrangement of services and appliances (see page 84), many also have to provide space for dining. Here it is important to keep the dining area out of the main kitchen traffic; an alcove is ideal. Stools pulled up to a counter are never very comfortable. I prefer a circular table with chairs set back into a corner, or a built-in banquette.

Bathrooms

Bathroom arrangements, similarly, depend on the positioning of the bathtub, lavatory and wash-basin (see page 87). But if the room is large enough, it is always good to promote a furnished atmosphere by including a chair or an upholstered stool and a sidetable.

Halls

Although for the sake of simplicity and safety the hall must not be cluttered, a table, however small, is essential. In a rectangular area, a rectangular table set back against a wall can be used as a bar table; in a circular, square or octagonal hall, a circular table in the middle of the room can be used to carry magazines, a plant or a large decorative

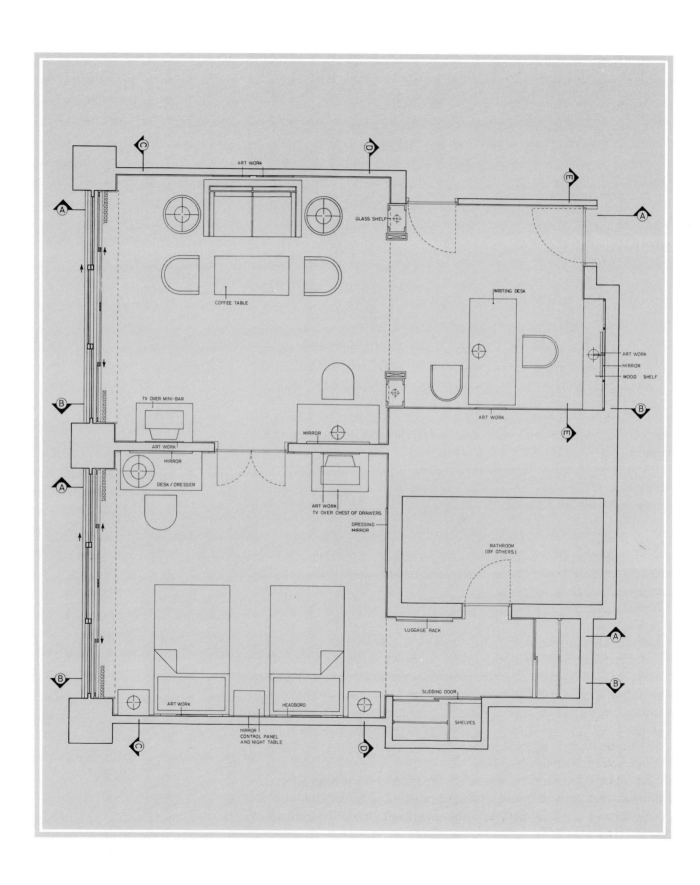

Left Two boardroom tables used side by side join handsomely together because of the design of the corner detail.

Far left Furniture layout for a suite in the Okura Hotel in Tokyo.

object. If the hall is big enough, the table can also be used for dinner parties.

Storage for coats is best when it is built-in. One neat solution is to form a recess by making a pair of cupboards. This space can then be used to house the hall table.

Public contracts

I choose the same type of furniture for public spaces and offices as I do for residential use, to promote style and comfort and prevent a clinical, ready-made look. In my own office, around a modern boardroom table, I have four Louis-XV-style chairs in natural beech, new interpretations but extremely elegant and comfortable. For general office use, there are many excellent and practical chair designs on the market.

In restaurants, chair design needs careful thought. Chairs must be attractive, original and hard-wearing; they also must be competitively priced. I often find that straight-backed upholstered chairs fulfil most requirements. Positioning of tables must be planned to promote a sense of space without isolating each party. Building partitions or stalls to enclose each table can increase privacy but is inflexible; a combination of open seating and stalls may work well.

In foyers and reception areas, seating for visitors must be comfortable and the atmosphere as welcoming as possible. The desk must be discreetly designed so that the control panel is not visible. (For office layout see page 80.)

CHAPTER EIGHT

FINISHING TOUCHES

The importance of detail cannot be overestimated. The best decorating and furnishing can be let down by an ugly radiator, badly hung pictures or poorly displayed objects. It is on this level that a room finally works or doesn't, has vitality or is lifeless.

Details are just as important to a room as accessories are to a dress. A suit is not complete without a tie, but the tie must be well-knotted and straight; a plain dress may call for a brooch, but the brooch must be pinned in the right position. In the same way, it is not just what objects a room contains, but how they are arranged.

As well as selection and display, attention to detail may demand the opposite strategy – disguise. Few homes are perfect and few budgets large enough to make them so. Visual trickery can make inharmonious features recede, and bring out what is best in a room.

As in other areas of design, imagination and ingenuity count for more than spending power. Flowers, for example, immediately breathe life into a room, and a collection of beach stones, well arranged, can be just as interesting as a valuable piece of sculpture.

Far right In an old house in the Channel Islands I accepted the naive charm of a beam running through the middle of the bedroom, and aligned the dressing table along this axis, making a virtue out of what could have been an obstacle.

DISGUISE

Since the late nineteenth century there has been a strand of thinking in design which has promoted honesty of form and materials above all else, eschewing not only disguise, but also almost all forms of decoration. This attitude has, at times, been so pervasive that cosmetic treatments have been seen as a kind of cheating.

This is a misconception. Disguise in an interior is not about dishonesty or fakery, but concerns emphasis and practicality. Many rooms contain awkward features, which can be eyesores if left exposed. Others may be inherently badly proportioned. The art of the interior designer is to change the emphasis so that what should be the focus of attention is brought out. This is not just a question of aesthetics: for example, if it is not structurally or financially possible to improve the quality of a space by substantial remodelling, disguise in the form of a tented ceiling, new cornice or false alcove can help.

Adjusting proportions

If a room is badly proportioned – too tall, too narrow, too low – changing the structure may be ruled out for reasons of cost or practicality. But there are strategies you can adopt to improve matters, many of which are inexpensive.

In some homes, poor conversion may have resulted in awkwardly shaped spaces. For example, if a high-ceilinged room has been divided, the two new areas created may appear taller than the floor area would warrant. The solution here may be to add false ceilings to bring down the height of the rooms. Since ceilings are merely applied to the underside of floors, this is not a structural change, nor very expensive to execute.

Low rooms, on the other hand, need some form of vertical emphasis. This can be provided by curtains which extend right up to the cornice, or by building floor-to-ceiling cupboards, or even by covering the walls in a vertically striped wallpaper.

Narrow rooms can be improved by using an expanse of mirror to add depth. Once, in a typically small New York bathroom, I mirrored all the walls and the ceiling, which produced a wonderfully sparkling and generous effect.

Window treatments can also be cosmetic. Squat windows can be heightened with deep pelmets, narrow windows widened with full curtains. In my London office the window is unattractive and metal-framed and the view of the building opposite uninspiring. To soften both the view and the harsh lines of the window I added a grille made of natural wood. This also serves to hide the radiator below the window sill.

A structural beam, column or boxed-in stack carrying pipework can also present a difficult element. The lack of symmetry is often what makes such features irksome. One of my current commissions involves

re-doing 600 bedrooms for a Tokyo hotel, all of which have extremely awkward vertical and horizontal beams. The uprights will be lost by forming alcoves for the beds and bedside tables; the horizontal beams will be played down by adding cornices.

Concealment

Radiators, heating ducts, fans and vents often strike a jarring note in the interior. During the nineteenth century radiators were often disguised in most elaborate ways. Later, in the 1930s, it was fashionable in modern houses to expose the radiator as a feature, a trend that has continued to the present day. However, traditional designers never deviated from the Victorian principle and continued to disguise radiators with wooden grilles, wire mesh and pleated silk panels.

I do not find that radiators make any contribution to the style of the room and prefer wherever possible to cover them. For Lord and Lady Londonderry I conceived a design for radiator covers which was adapted from a fretwork detail in the dairy at Woburn Abbey. I paint such a cover the same colour as the woodwork in the room, but the radiator and interior of the case are matt black, or very dark brown. I often place four-fold screens slightly higher than the radiator itself, in front of it. Made of plain wood painted to match the wall colour or covered with fabric, they are inexpensive and elegant.

Concealment can also add to the coherence of a room. This is particularly true of concealed, or 'jib' doors. My London hall is a small space, about ten feet by four feet, and, besides the front door, there are three doors leading to different rooms. Since none of the doors could be blocked up without losing access, I decided to conceal two of them in an attempt to make the space seem less claustrophobic. The kitchen door is covered with a set of prints; the bedroom door has a table, picture and picture light fixed to it, which open with the door. In my country dining room, where the walls are covered with a mural, I have jibbed both doors and the serving hatch to keep the continuity of the painting.

Jib doors can be simple or extremely complicated, depending on the degree of sophistication required. Some only need to be finished to blend in with the wall; I have seen others which incorporate real books on bookshelves. I even designed an external jib door for a house in Provence, which was then covered with Virginia creeper from the hinged side.

Sometimes, however, concealment is not possible, and in such situations lateral thinking can be of enormous benefit. My Paris associate, Christian Badin, once had to accommodate a large fire-hose and two extinguishers in the design of an office corridor. His solution was to construct a frame around them which was lined with brilliant cobalt blue, and display the scarlet fire equipment as a modern treasure – a witty solution.

DISPLAY

Interesting objects, well arranged, make all the difference to a room. Even the starkest modern interior needs a few pieces that are not strictly functional, but are there solely for the purpose of enjoyment – of their colour, texture, content or provenance. Objects can also add a sense of surprise, enthusiasm and style, a personal touch which prevents a room from looking sterile and unlived-in.

Whatever you are displaying, from antique toys to watercolours, there are a number of guidelines to bear in mind. The most important is to mass your possessions – do not dot them about so their impact is lost. A group, linked by colour, theme or texture, has infinitely more visual value than the same collection scattered about the room. Arrange pieces so they are connected in some way and add to one another. Spend time determining the best arrangement: don't just clutter all the objects in one place and hope for the best, or range them in dull, geometric rows. Treat the display as an exercise in composition, with the aim of achieving a result that looks effortless and natural.

Museums can be a good source of inspiration. Not long ago, museum displays were a byword for lack of imagination. Nowadays, however, major exhibitions and national collections are often sensitively designed and laid out, and much can be learned from them. I am always intrigued to compare the work of different curators. Where one will achieve a result that is abundant in warmth, wit and imagination, another will simply lay out the collection for inspection: a bland method of display.

With a few notable exceptions, many private collectors have had much more knowledge than taste, and it is exciting to see, a few years after collections have been bequeathed to a museum or the National Trust, the contents organized and displayed with great flair in a new setting. Perhaps the best example of this is the Gulbenkian collection, now housed in a new building in Lisbon and looking superb: infinitely better than it has ever looked before.

'Tablescapes'

I coined the term 'tablescape' twenty years ago to define a collection of objects and flowers arranged on a tabletop or similar surface. Since that time, tablescapes have become a distinctive feature of my style of interior decoration.

I learned much of what I know about arranging objects from friends such as Roderick Cameron and Winnie Portarlington, both of whom delighted in collecting and had a genius for display. Rory Cameron was a great traveller and loved to arrange the pieces he had collected from around the world. One of his most memorable tablescapes, now, alas, dispersed, included a Greek marble foot, four blue-green Egyptian Anubises, a pair of Roman iridescent glass bottles and two large pieces of turquoise from Turkestan.

Left Red leather tooled 'Freedom' cases look statuesque on a porphyry surface.

Above far left A collection of silver eggs grouped in bowls on a mahogany table-top.

Below far left Two Chinese cockerels and a pair of Chinese pink elephants parade beneath a model of Giotto's tower. A Turkish gilded bronze helmet stands in front of a Nevers vase.

Winnie Portarlington had a whimsical way with table settings. A favourite consisted of snuff boxes at each person's place, with silver pug dogs in a circle in front of her own. Her grandson continues the same tradition today in his house in Australia.

The most exciting tablescapes I have ever seen, however, were in the Santa Barbara home of an American collector. When I visited Wright Luddington's house I was only twenty-four and my ideas about composition were chiefly derived from still-life paintings. Here I saw something vastly more stimulating. The living room was a resolutely plain, modern double cube, with raw, plaster walls and a tray ceiling rising out of a huge cornice. There were no pictures, but at either end of the room two large alcoves housed classical statues from Lansdowne House. Opposite the window wall was a massive stone chimney, flanked by two enormous console tables. These held every kind of object, all related by colour, texture or material. One collection, I remember, was of seventeenth-century Venetian glass, another Aztec pottery. But within each arrangement there was always a surprise. Among the Venetian glass one would suddenly spot a piece of Lalique; among the pottery, a ripe gourd.

Tablescapes can be made on any surface – side or sofa tables, console tables and dining tables, but also shelves, chimney-pieces, dressing tables and commodes. The chimney-piece is an obvious place for display. The traditional arrangement is a pair of candlesticks flanking an antique clock, all set below a classical mirror. However, there is no need to adhere to such a pattern. I often make asymmetrical groupings, placing a pair of objects to one side, balanced by a flower arrangement.

When objects are grouped on a tabletop, they should be related in colour or texture, and enough room should be allowed for ashtrays and glasses. A yellow pottery table lamp, for example, might inspire an arrangement of yellow, brass, orange and amber objects, or flowers.

In my house in the South of France, I made two tablescapes on glass-topped tables, each lit from below by an uplighter. One consisted of a collection of inexpensive but old clear glass – wine glasses, beakers and a small carafe – and the other was a group of old blue chemist's bottles in different shapes and sizes.

In my bedroom in the country, I have surrounded myself with objects that hold great personal meaning, arranged in illuminated cabinets. I have mechanical toys from my childhood, a coffee cup salvaged from the blitz, a collection of penknives and a cigarette box I painted as a schoolboy, none of them valuable in themselves, but all things which provoke memories and interest. In the same way, anyone can assemble their own *objets trouvés*, even on the lowest budget.

The most precious or dramatic elements in a collection can be given added impact by mounting them or covering them with perspex cases. This not only directs attention to them, but prevents damage and saves dusting. I once assembled a collection of ivory pieces from different

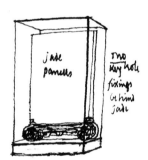

jade panels

two key hole fixings behind jade

Bases to be repaired in Wallingford : same single chair back

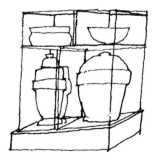

+ Dng room bowls

Left A gloriously disparate collection of crystal, glass, jade, tin and silver objects on a glass-topped table makes a reflective and enjoyable display group.

Below A cream Neapolitan vase dominates a collection of family snapshots and diverse objects, including a Byzantine lady, a Renaissance paten and an early-nineteenth-century Wedgwood mug.

periods and parts of the world for an American client living in Wiltshire, and then devised a series of boxes, cubes and solid cylinders in perspex as display plinths. All were at different heights to provide variety and, to introduce even more interest, I covered one of the stands in chamois leather, one in silver leaf and made another out of ivory-coloured perspex.

Themes are always intriguing. A table full of heads in bronze, terracotta, porcelain, silver gilt or carved wood or a collection of obelisks in different materials and different scales would be exciting.

The purpose of a tablescape is to add life to an interior. Consequently it should be flexible, permitting rearrangement, addition or even replacement. Some of my clients have not fully appreciated this point. I once decorated an apartment on Fifth Avenue for a New York couple, and, during the course of my work, assembled a collection of Roman heads for the chimney-piece, which I then arranged asymmetrically. When I returned to the apartment a year later, I was tempted to move one of the pieces to improve upon the arrangement. To my surprise, I discovered a square neatly painted on the mantelpiece to indicate exactly where the object should be replaced after dusting!

Right For Paul Channon, before he became Secretary of State for Trade and Industry, I arranged a collection of Meissen birds on brackets, each lit by a bulb concealed in the bracket. Both the brackets and the walls were covered with claret-coloured velvet.

Far right Between two imposing but rather heavy-looking portraits, a group of nineteenth-century drawings lightens the effect.

Wall display

Objects mounted on walls can look particularly dramatic. As with tablescapes, you should group what you are displaying to maximize impact.

When I was asked to display a collection of Aztec gold in a room in Chelsea, I stretched dark cedar-green silk velvet on the walls and mounted the gold objects on perspex in perspex vitrines, each lit with a tiny bulb. I have also mounted Meissen figures on claret, velvet-covered brackets, with built-in lights again, on walls covered with the same shade of velvet. Both effects are stunning at night. For the second Earl Beatty at Chicheley Hall, I mounted his famous father's medals and decorations on black velvet and put them into twelve burnished gold-leaf box frames, each with a picture light.

Bookshelves should also be treated as much as an exercise in display as storage. Be generous with shelving and try to fill the space as much as you can, with magazines and paperbacks if necessary. Wherever possible, line the entire wall with books to give a cosy, lived-in look. Old bindings and modern dustjackets can add a richness of colour and texture.

Hanging pictures

When exhibiting pictures of any kind, there are several aspects to consider: the position of the picture on the wall, how it is fixed and the type of frame used to display it. A simple rule of thumb is that pictures should be hung so that the centre is at eye level. Small pictures look well grouped. There are exceptions. I have recently commissioned two large modern paintings for a lofty room in Cambridge, Massachusetts. When I discussed with the artist how these should best be displayed, I suggested that they could be hung one above another to take advantage of the scale of the room, a novel approach he had not considered, but willingly accepted.

A group of pictures should be united by theme or content, or by medium, or both. A set of architectural prints, for example, or watercolour studies, have much more style placed together than they would in isolation. In an average-sized living room, hanging a picture on each wall is not nearly as interesting as displaying a pair on either side of the chimney breast, and a group on the opposite wall.

Picture rails are unattractive except in a Victorian interior. Always use two fixings as wide apart as possible to keep the picture stable and flat. A superb antique painting can be centrally displayed, and supported by a wide velvet or grosgrain band trimmed with a rosette – a flourish that makes a feature out of the hanging and looks luxurious.

Old paintings of quality are really the only pictures that merit elaborate gessoed and gilded frames. Prints and drawings have a crispness that is best accentuated by the simple lines of plain or painted wooden or metal frames, or box frames with glass clipped to the front.

Modern paintings, especially abstract ones, are best unframed, the rough edge of the canvas supplying definition.

Accessories

Every interior inevitably includes a host of incidental objects and details that could be loosely termed accessories. Wastepaper baskets, ashtrays, soap dishes, light switches, toothbrushes, doorknobs, hand-towels, window latches and lavatory paper are all everyday necessities, often in full view, and all too often glaringly ill-considered.

These minor details can assume much more importance than they warrant if they are not chosen correctly. It costs no more to coordinate towels, lavatory paper and toothbrushes with the colour of the bathroom decoration, and the result is immediately stylish and considered. A large pottery ashtray has an honest, forthright style that is much more successful than several small, ornate cut-glass ones.

Similarly, pay attention to door and window fittings. The simplest ironmongery is often the best. A first selection can be made from manufacturers' catalogues or advertisements placed in trade magazines. Avoid the fussy, over-styled versions – they are often impractical in use as well as distracting to the eye.

Switches and socket plates should also be well designed but unobtrusive. The modern plastic varieties are cheap and ubiquitous, but styleless; unfortunately, neater fittings in better materials tend to be expensive.

Left The importance of detail: clear perspex door handles look handsome on plate-glass doors.

Flowers

Flowers are the ultimate finishing touch. They provide colour, shape, and vitality. And most importantly, they link the interior with the world outside, by reflecting the mood of different seasons and landscapes.

I believe that only someone who grows their own plants can fully appreciate how to arrange flowers. For this reason, among others, I prefer real garden flowers to hothouse varieties. I particularly abhor commercial roses. But if you lack a garden, window boxes, containers or even a sunny roof terrace can all provide a reasonable amount of flowers.

I have a small greenhouse where white jasmine grows alongside a geranium on the back wall. The jasmine provides delicious nosegays from late October to March. I also have roses and various geraniums growing here in pots for use in the house. And in January I dig up a

Right On a pair of fine Louis XV console tables I set two dramatic arrangements of dried flowers in galvanized-iron buckets.

Far right In my London apartment an abstract head by John Wragg and a seventeenth-century lead head of Mercury sit on a Louis XVI table, the composition illuminated by an electrified candlestick.

Far left In my bedroom in the country, two glazed Gothic cupboards on either side of the bed are full of memorabilia, creating a personal ambience.

Above left The bath alcove in my country bedroom is lined with Directoire prints which depict medieval artefacts. The collection is arranged, for maximum impact, to read as a single group.

Below left These clients had beautiful possessions and when I was rearranging their entire house, I was able to say where objects were best sited. I composed a formal, controlled arrangement centred on the Louis XV fireplace. A late-eighteenth-century looking-glass reflects the Kolsa oil chandelier in front; a magnificent Louis XVI clock is flanked by two Sèvres cache-pots, which in turn are flanked by two Louis XV candlestick appliqués which I de-electrified. To the extreme left and right are two more porcelain cache-pots on pedestals.

spadeful of snowdrops from the garden, when the buds are just beginning, pot them and bring them indoors. Once the flowers have bloomed, the bulbs are replanted outside.

Flower arrangements should always be seasonal. Summer is naturally the high point, with an abundance and variety of species at the peak of flowering: mass the blooms using colour to complement or contrast with the decorative scheme in a particular room. In winter, dried flowers such as hydrangeas and gypsophylla, and interesting foliage such as bergenia leaves, dried grass and seed heads, are very attractive, massed in the same way as fresh arrangements. In early spring and autumn, when there are few blooms, single flowers in a series of interesting containers look much more effective than a single bouquet in one vase.

A group of containers in different styles and shapes, holding different flowers of varying heights, both growing and cut, but linked by colour can be extremely interesting. Containers are very important. Simple shapes in materials such as pottery, earthenware, glass, pewter and basketwork are far better than over-decorated varieties. Pack flowers in upright cylinders for fullness; mass them in low troughs or tanks for a carpet of colour in the middle of a dining table. My favourite containers are two-inch perspex cylinders, actually the containers in which the film for my camera is sold. I often trim roses very short and place a single bloom each in six or eight of these cylinders and arrange them in a grid about six inches apart. The effect is arresting – as if the flowers were floating on the surface.

A display of greenery can be just as refreshing as a stunning flower arrangement. Quite humble species can give much textural interest, as well as providing wonderful scents. I have a favourite lemon-scented geranium, now three feet high, which winters in my drawing room. Many houseplants have a graphic quality that lends interest to a modern room: *Ficus lyrata* can be very handsome in this respect. But I dislike all plants that are variegated – they seem indecisive to me – and I would never have a rubber plant, even in a sub-tropical garden.

Far left White flowers add life to this collection of objects on a marble-topped table. The complementary colours and forms achieve a certain serenity.

GLOSSARY

Accent In a colour scheme, a vivid contrasting shade which counterpoints the basic decorative palette, such as shocking pink, with a series of reds.

Alcove A semi-circular or square recess, the base of which is at floor or chair-rail level; it can be of any depth up to seven feet.

Architect Professional specializing in the design and construction of buildings. Architects should be consulted for all internal reorganization which involves changes to a building's structure.

Architectural detail Decorative and non-structural interior trim, applied or built in to the surface of a wall, such as a cornice, chair rail or architrave.

Architrave Wooden, metal or plaster moulding framing a door, internal opening or window. Architraves are not purely decorative, as they hide the joint between the door frame and the wall. They may be plain, profiled or more elaborate in design.

Art Deco Style of decoration, furnishing and architecture popular in the 1920s and 1930s, relying on geometric, streamlined forms and expressed in materials such as glass, chrome and plastic.

Art Nouveau Style of decoration, furnishing and architecture arising out of the Arts and Crafts Movement of the late nineteenth century. Characterized by stylized, sinuous forms derived from nature.

Baroque Highly ornate but strong style of design and architecture prevalent in the seventeenth and early eighteenth centuries

Bergère A French chair, from any period between Louis XV and today, which has arms. The space between the padded elbows and the seat is upholstered, unlike a **fauteuil.**

Brief The process of consultation between client and professional, determining the nature of the job, and its financial, practical and personal parameters. The most important aspect of any job.

Brussels weave A type of carpet, woven with a tight, uncut loop pile, in which crisp, small geometric designs can happily be interpreted.

Café curtains Curtains suspended from a pole or rod halfway up a window, screening the lower portion; or a pair of curtains, one on top of the other. Café curtains can be made of a light, semi-transparent fabric and used in conjunction with full-length outer curtains.

Canisse French term for split cane woven into an openwork material, often used to shade outdoor terraces.

Casement window Window hinged along a vertical side, which opens like a door, inwards on the continent, so beware of curtain and blind fixings.

Ceiling rose Decorative plasterwork, usually in the centre of the ceiling, from which lighting fixtures are suspended. Though appearing much earlier, the ceiling rose is a typical Victorian architectural detail and often displays floral or leaf motifs.

Chair rail Decorative wooden moulding, set about thirty inches from the ground around the perimeter of the room. Traditionally used to protect fine wall finishes from damage caused by chair backs, hence the name.

Chimney-piece Decorative and protective surround for fireplace, almost always incorporating a shelf. Can be of virtually any date and be made of stone, marble, slate, wood, pottery or cast iron.

Chintz Printed cotton cloth used in furnishing, often glazed.

Circulation The flow of traffic from one room to another, or within a room, connecting common points. A study of circulation is important when designing seating plans, office layouts and structural remodelling.

Close covering Type of upholstery in which the fabric is stretched tight and fixed to the furniture frame. It can also mean wall-to-wall carpets.

Coir Cheap, practical matting made of coconut fibre, with an interesting, nubbly texture.

Commode Chest of drawers, of drawing-room quality, often with a marble top; not a bedroom chest of drawers.

Console table Small rectangular table which usually stands against a wall. It need only have two front legs, with the back of the table being fixed to the wall.

Cornice Decorative plasterwork moulding around the perimeter of the room between the wall and ceiling, forming a pleasing junction between the two planes. Designs vary from plain to highly elaborate.

Corona Circular or oval frame attached to the ceiling, from which bed drapery is hung. **Half-coronas** are semi-circular frames fixed back to a wall, with drapery extending down to the left, the right and behind the bedhead.

Damask Traditional furnishing fabric, often made of silk, with patterns woven in the material.

Dead light The spare margin of wall above the top of a window frame and below the cornice.

Dhurrie Traditional Indian woven carpet, made of cotton or silk, and featuring geometric designs, which I recoloured and designed with H.H. the Rajmata of Jaipur in the early 1960s.

Dimmer switch Type of light switch which enables light levels to be controlled. Provides a smooth gradation in light from very dim to bright. Also known as a rheostat switch.

Directoire Style of French furniture dating from the early nineteenth century.

Distemper Common household water-based paint, now no longer produced, which had a soft, chalky finish. It has been replaced by matt emulsion.

Distressing Ways of finishing walls or furniture to simulate aged or antique surfaces. Often involves special paint techniques such as sponging, stippling or ragging.

Downlighter Type of contemporary light fitting recessed or fixed to the ceilng, which directs light primarily downwards.

Dress curtains Curtains which do not draw but which can, inexpensively, give a soft look to a room.

Eggshell Type of oil-based paint, which dries to a mid-sheen finish. Can be used on walls or woodwork.

Elbow chair Mid-eighteenth-century chair design, with upholstered oval or square back and half-upholstered arms.

Elevation Scale drawing of the vertical elements of a building, section of a room or piece of furniture.

Ergonomics Study of the efficient use of a given area, related to the needs and movements of its users. Designers of office furniture or kitchen units, for example, study ergonomics to ascertain optimum heights and depths for work surfaces.

Estimate Financial projection of the cost of a job supplied by the contractor or professional to the client.

Façade The external appearance of a building, facing the street or open space.

Fauteuil Eighteenth-century French armchair, with carved frame, sometimes gilded or painted. It has upholstered arms, like the **bergère,** but is open below.

Festoon blinds Type of window dressing in which fabric is attached to a heading and reefs up in loops, forming ruched swags.

Festoon curtains These hang like ordinary curtains, but pull up by day in large swags.

Flocked wallpaper Wallpaper that has a raised patterned surface achieved by glueing on small particles of paper to create the effect of velvet.

Fluorescent Type of light source produced by the fluorescence of gas, commonly in tubes, but also in bulbs. Depending on the type of bulb, it may have a marked greenish or pinkish tinge. I detest it in any area.

Gainsborough chair Mahogany-framed, eighteenth-century English armchair with upholstered armrests, so named because Gainsborough posed his sitters in this style of chair.

Georgian Period of furniture-making, decoration and architecture spanning the eighteenth century and characterized by neo-classical interpretations, refined proportions and fine workmanship.

Gloss Type of oil-based paint which dries to a high sheen. Traditionally used for woodwork and externally.

Gothic Medieval style of church architecture, characterized by arched windows, flying buttresses and vaulted ceilings. It was revived and reinterpreted in the mid-eighteenth and throughout the early nineteenth century.

Greek tombstone Regency decorative flourish for tops of wardrobes, sideboards and so on, copied by cabinet-makers from designs on Greek funerary urns in the British Museum.

Halogen Type of light source which produces a crisp, white light and is often used in modern **uplighters**.

Hessian Coarsely woven cloth made of jute. It is interesting to print an early design on it.

Holland blind Simple roller blind, consisting of flat, stiffened fabric fixed to a wooden roller and hung from brackets on either side of the window frame.

Interlining A soft layer of fabric stitched between the curtain material and the lining to make curtains hang well and to insulate against draughts.

Interior decorator Professional who specializes in creating a new decorative scheme using existing furniture, objects and interior spaces.

Interior designer Professional who creates entirely new interiors, by remodelling, commissioning new furniture and adding architectural detail.

Jib door Concealed door, specially hinged and hung so that it disappears into the wall when closed. Decorated like the wall, it is sometimes possible to increase the illusion by hanging prints on it.

Kelim A woven carpet or rug without pile, typically produced in Afghanistan. Look for ones in pale, unobtrusive colours.

Knole sofa Type of sofa with an upright back and cantilevered sides which let down. Dates from the seventeenth century and is thought to be the earliest sofa design. There are still original ones at Knole.

Lacquer A type of varnish applied in many layers to furniture or surfaces and polished to a deep sheen.

Layout A sketch or scale plan showing the arrangement of furniture, work spaces, rooms, etc.

Lighting plan Scale drawing made to show position of light fittings, sockets and switches.

Loose covering Tailored, removable covers for sofas and armchairs.

Louvres Angled, slatted strips of overlapping wood used in shutters or door panels to let in light but provide privacy.

Marbling (marblizing) Process of simulating real marble on a wall or other surface, using illusionist paint techniques.

Matt Non-reflective paint finish.

Modern movement Architectural style of the early twentieth century which rejected the influence of the past and relied on undecorated, cubic forms, white plain surfaces, concrete, and either large or very small windows.

Moulding Decorative wooden or plaster trim.

Neo-classical Style of architecture current in the late eighteenth century and based on a revival of classical forms. It can also be applied to the Greek revival movement in the Regency period.

Pediment Triangular section of wall over an entrance, portico, or window or forming the gable end of a roof; similar flourish on free-standing furniture.

Pelmet Border or valance at the top of a window frame to cover the curtain heading. May be shaped or plain, made of fabric-covered wood or fabric. Pelmets are also used to cover the frame of a tester bed.

Perspective drawing Artist's rendering of a proposed interior, building, etc., set up in perspective to give a lifelike impression of the eventual result.

Petersham ribbon Thick ribbed silk ribbon used as a decorative trimming.

Picture light Oblong, metal shaded light which projects over a picture to light it.

Picture rail A wooden moulding set three-quarters of the way up the wall, devised during Victorian times as a means of suspending pictures.

Plan Scale drawing of the horizontal plane of a room, seating arrangement, floor of a building.

Ragging Technique of applying paint using a rag to dab colour on or off the wall, leaving a characteristic, textured imprint.

Regency Style of decoration and furnishing dating from the early nineteenth century and revived immediately after the Second World War. The furniture was extremely delicate and refined, with antiquarian Egyptian and Greek influences.

Roman blind Fabric blind attached to a batten, which pulls up vertically in pleats by means of cords running along the underside of the blind.

Sash window Window in two halves, which slide up and down on vertical runners by means of a sash cord.

Scagliola Plaster, dye and marble chips mixed with glue to imitate marble. Used internally only.

Scale drawing Any drawing which reproduces actual proportions and spatial relationships, based on dimensions of the area concerned. For example, a drawing made at a scale of 1:10 would represent elements at one tenth their real size.

Scheme board Samples of decorative treatments – wall colours, fabrics, carpets – for different rooms assembled on one display card which can be put together with others so the whole apartment or house schemes can be seen in relation to each other.

Services All the technical facilities – water, drainage, electricity, heating, air conditioning – that supply a building.

Skirting board Wooden strip applied around the perimeter of a room at floor level, protecting the base of the wall from damage and providing a visual junction between the wall and the floor.

Slub weave An uneven fabric weave with obvious irregularities, producing a textured effect, such as in raw silk.

Sponging Paint technique which involves using a natural or marine sponge to dab colour on or off a surface, producing a mottled, textural effect.

Spotlight Type of light fitting, wall- or ceiling-mounted or free-standing, which gives a concentrated, directable beam of light.

Standard light Floor-standing upright lamp; with metal shades can be very elegant.

Stippling Paint technique in which colour is flicked on a surface using the end of a stiff brush, producing a speckled, textural effect.

Striplight Wall- or ceiling-mounted light fixture, usually fitted with a fluorescent tube.

Structural alteration Any change to the basic elements of a building, such as the walls, roof, floors, which has an effect on the way the building stands up or holds together.

Sub-contractor Supplier or skilled worker employed by the main contractor or professional to provide specialist services, such as plumbing or masonry.

Suspended ceiling False ceiling, applied beneath original, to lower the height of a room or conceal services such as pipework or ducts.

Swagged drapery Window treatment in which fabric is elaborately draped above the window frame and is framed by tails of fabric.

Swan chair Bucket-shaped chair with swan-headed arms, after a famous Directoire set at Malmaison.

Tablescape Decorative arrangement of objects, flowers, sculpture, etc., on a table-top or similar surface.

Tallboy High chest of drawers on turned legs, a style dating from the seventeenth century.

Tented ceiling Fabric covering a ceiling, gathered to a central point.

Tester bed Draped bed, formed by attaching a rectangular framework to the ceiling and suspending curtains from each of the four corners with a pelmet.

Ticking Striped linen or cotton fabric used to cover bedding.

Tole Painted metal objects, especially light fittings, made in France.

Tungsten Most common domestic light source, produced by an incandescent filament in a glass bulb. Tungsten light has a yellowish tinge which makes it sympathetic in the interior.

Uplighter Free-standing or wall-mounted light fitting which directs light primarily at the ceiling.

Venetian blind Slatted metal or wooden blinds, available in different widths and colours, which can be adjusted to control the amount of light filtered through the window.

Walling Fabric stretched over a wall and nailed to battens. The fabric is usually interlined to give a smooth, taut surface.

Wall washer Type of spotlight which bathes an area of wall rather than a single part of it.

Wilton Type of carpet, with a cut pile.

INDEX